The
Consciousness
Paradigm

John Smotherman

The

Consciousness

Paradigm

The Consciousness Paradigm

ISBN 13: 978-0-6153679-3-4
ISBN 10: 0-6153679-3-3
LCCN: 2010926804

OCC014000 BODY, MIND & SPIRIT / New Thought
OCC019000 BODY, MIND & SPIRIT / Inspiration & Personal Growth

First Edition
1 2 3 4 5 6 7 8 9 10

This is a Wisdom House product, published by Wisdom House Books.
For information, please contact:
Wisdom House Books
15455 Dallas Parkway, Suite 600
Dallas, Texas 75001
Tel. 972-764-3222
Contact the author at John@AppliedConsciousnessSystems.com
www.wisdomhousebooks.com

Special Thanks

This effort is the compilation of the wisdom and contributions of many sources and many amazing people. I want to especially thank the following individuals who, through their experiences, insights, time, and energy, have made immeasurable contributions to my life and this work. In chronological order, they are

Andrew Schliesser

Andrew Schultz

Cindy Smotherman

Natalie Fletcher

Charlette Mann

Laura Rose

Vaughan Wynne-Jones

Shannon Looper

Charlie McIntyre

Daniel D'Neuville

Michael McElhenie

Thanks to my editors, Tricia Allen and Deanne Lachner, to whom I'm grateful for their hard and tireless work as well as their gentleness and patience with me. Thanks also to Ted Ruybal for his design work. Special thanks to Chung for her support and sacrifices so that this book could be published. Most especially I want to thank my amazing wife, Cindy, who is a beautiful, old soul and a radiant, young woman. She was the first person I ever met who also saw what I saw. She believed in me and supported me through thick and thin. Without her steadfast love and unwavering support, this book would not have been possible. Truly, it was a team effort. Last, but not least, thank you to all who read this book with an open mind and heart and a view toward improving our world.

Contents

Contents

Preface

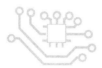

I was challenged by my editor to explain why I wrote this book. In short, this book is my life's work. The journey of my life has been, by and large, a quest to solve two riddles:

1) "How can I make the greatest contribution I am capable of toward making the world a better place?"

2) "How can we, as individuals, best secure happiness in our lives?"

After years and years of studying ancient and modern wisdom, of personal investigation and experimentation, of gruelingly deep and frank discussions with other people, and of keen observation of the lives of those around me, I came to the discovery of my life: the solution to both those challenges is one and the same—raise consciousness.

In writing this book, I endeavor to make the greatest contribution to the world of which I am capable. In its pages, I focus attention on raising consciousness, which I believe is the greatest fulcrum for leveraging the world into a better place for everyone. It makes the case that truly empathizing with all of humanity is one of the most fulfilling things we can do. It gives life a gravity of meaning and purpose that fulfills us at levels the ego cannot reach. This book also makes the case that it is the mindset of the world at large that holds the greatest immediate hope and potential boon to people who live in the most desperate of circumstances. We have the means to alleviate extreme poverty and the desperation and ills associated with it. It is a question of mustering the concern and will to do it. It is also the mindset of the world at large that will, more than anything else, determine the kind of Earth our children and our children's children will inherit.

This book is also an outgrowth of my own search for happiness. My story begins in East Texas in the mid-1960s. I am, in many ways, the average person. I was born to a middle class family in a mid-sized town in the middle of the United States. As I grew and entered school, I also regularly attended Sunday school classes at the Methodist church my family attended. I was taught all kinds of fascinating stories about interesting individuals. I was taught about morality and God and Jesus and how they wanted me to live my life. I was taught to ignore what I thought were obvious inconsistencies within the Bible. I was further troubled and mystified by the hypocrisies that appeared to me to be endemic in the religious lifestyle. During my first year in high school, I spiraled into depression as I contemplated all the bad things in the world and wrestled with how God could allow them. I sank even deeper as I realized, to my horror, that those things also lived within me. I began a desperate search for knowledge and understanding.

By the time I was sixteen, I was struck with the conviction that something had to be done to improve the world and make it a better, happier, more loving place. I was also struck to my core with the conviction that, in some way, I had to contribute to this endeavor. In some way and in some portion, the responsibility was mine, yet I had no idea how to even begin going about it. So with no clue or direction about how I was supposed to approach this "mission" or even what specifically my "mission" was, I went to college and then to law school.

As a lawyer, I practiced family law for eleven years. Clients came to me for help in getting divorces and in dealing with child custody and support issues. Family law is an emotionally charged area of the law, and most calls I received were from people who were crying, screaming, or merely at their wits' end. My clients were really good people in really difficult circumstances. But I came to understand that my role as a family lawyer was like that of a pilot who was repeatedly teleported into planes that were crashing. There was no avoiding the crash; the best I could possibly do was lessen the damage and loss of life. Immediately after I finished one crash, I would be teleported into the next. I began to see a pattern in clients' behavior that I found troubling. Oftentimes, the true cause of their difficulties was within themselves, but most were unable to face that difficult fact. They always perceived the source of their trouble as being in the spouse/ex-spouse, the judge, or the lawyers. It was never themselves.

The true source of my clients' difficulties sprang from weaknesses within themselves. These weaknesses ran the gamut of those that all of us as humans have. I was able to recognize them because I had come face to face with them in myself and had fought many personal battles with them. I learned firsthand and from witnessing clients' self-imposed struggles how our weaknesses in thinking and beliefs about ourselves and the world create misery. I knew too well the depth of pain our weaknesses can cause because I had experienced that pain so many times. It is these weaknesses we must acknowledge and overcome if we want to have truly exceptional and happy lives. As one example, in my practice I saw a common self-defense mechanism among clients. Most of my clients claimed their spouse/ex was a monster and the cause of all the trouble. However, the unacknowledged fact remained that the client had at one time chosen that monster. If clients finished their divorces believing that the cause of all the difficulty was the spouse, they would never face the weaknesses within themselves that caused them to choose a monster in the first place. These individuals would never improve their skills for choosing a mate and, consequently, would soon choose another monster. This same principle applied to friction that my clients had caused or con-tributed to within relationships. Never open to being a cause or even a contributor, my clients would not change themselves, and they would therefore never succeed in eliminating that friction. I saw this cycle repeat itself over and over. When all the blame was tossed on the other side, instead of my clients taking responsibility for their contributions, the problems would soon surface again in another context, presumably caused by someone else. Thus, my clients would doom themselves to never having a better experience of life than they were presently having.

On a (very) few occasions, I had the privilege of observing that rare client who looked at everything in terms of what he or she had contributed to the problem and how to improve to keep from repeating the same mistakes in the future. Invariably, these clients would continuously improve themselves and, as a result, the lives they experienced. But these were the rare exceptions. The vast majority of people fell in the first category. Over and over, I tried suggesting that they take a look inside themselves to see what they could improve. Invariably, they would go on the defensive, feeling that I was attacking them instead of defending them as their advocate. They would completely miss the fact that I was trying to help them. Because honest self-analysis is often painful, all they could see was the pain.

As a result of patterns I saw repeated over and over, I came to the conviction that, as a family lawyer, I was not really helping people. At least not in the way I wanted to. I was assisting clients through their legal cases, but I knew they would soon be experiencing the same unpleasantness again. It might recur in their next relationship, it might recur in other circumstances, but it would recur. It would return again and again, in many different manifestations, until they addressed the portion of the cause that was within themselves. Without changing themselves, their results in the future were unlikely to improve. My deepest desire was to provide a method for people to escape and not have to experience such unpleasantness in the future. I did not want to provide just a transition, I wanted to provide a solution. In short, what I really wanted to do was more than simply help people get through their immediate crises, I wanted to empower them to avoid getting themselves into similar circumstances in the future. I wanted to empower people to create better lives for themselves. I wanted to uncover and understand the mechanics of how to be, and stay, truly happy. Over the years, I began to focus on what I observed to be the most logical and reliable means of accomplishing this: raising people's consciousness.

I spent many years scouring the halls of human wisdom, learning the secrets of what makes us happy and unhappy. Consciousness became my preoccupation. I was fascinated at how many aspects of our lives it is connected to. I began to look at consciousness and patterns of consciousness across individuals and institutions. I studied its activity and evolution through history. I saw that certain mental skills were heralded again and again through history as reliable means of escaping and remaining free from the prison of pain. I observed that a large number of the greatest contributors to humanity's welfare and evolution were staunch advocates of many of these same skills. It eventually appeared to me that consciousness was evolving, and we were evolving with it. Today, we are at the beginning of an evolutionary step forward for consciousness, a revolution of sorts.

It was, and is, my deepest desire to liberate people from so much of the unnecessary pain and unhappiness I see in the world, and to free the disadvantaged from the grueling circumstances that make life so difficult for them. Moreover, I want to provide tools and understanding to aid people in securing for themselves the life of their dreams. My aim in writing this book is to provide a synthesized summary, a condensed guidebook, of our cumulative wisdom on how to have and experience the life we most desire. In short, it boils down to how we order our minds. In the simplest of terms, life is all about converting energy into happiness. The mind is the machine that makes that conversion. This book seeks to train the mind to achieve that goal in the most effective and efficient manner possible.

Introduction

From Consciousness to Happiness

onsciousness is the most pressing issue of our time. More than anything else, it determines the levels of happiness and success that we attain as individuals, the amount of war and poverty we have in the world, and the measure of the destruction we do to the planet. We are on the brink of a seismic shift in human consciousness. Our concept of who and what we are as humans is going to be shaken and reordered. Many subtle telltale signs indicate this, as do some glaringly obvious ones. Three main trends that point to this change are

1. the converging aspects of science and spirituality;

2. the emergence of a self-assertive, collective consciousness;

3. the historically unprecedented shift in the conscious perspectives of many people across the globe.

While these three trends are deeply linked to each other, for analytical purposes, we will look at them individually. They are like three continents gliding in a continental drift that will soon bring them to an earth-trembling collision. This collision will bring many changes and produce a new world unlike any that has been seen before. Although temporarily disorienting for many, and quite stressful for some, this natural phenomenon will be a good one. It will mark a significant step toward creating a better world.

One aspect of this book that bears consideration is its free flowing perspective changes and paradigm shifts. For instance, many religions have similar principles: rules for behavior, a belief in an afterlife, and reliance on a supreme being. Once the surface elements are stripped away and the essence of what they teach is revealed and compared, there is remarkable commonality. All seem to agree that love is the glue that holds man together, living solely for oneself is an empty life, and man ought to aspire to and behave at the height of his capabilities.

In many other fields, common thoughts and ideas, when wrapped in the trappings of different cultures, appear not to be similar. It is as if we attend a play in which one actor plays many parts. While some will focus on the costumes (cultural trappings) and miss the actor, others will focus on the actor and recognize him in his many guises. This book will endeavor to examine the actor, and in doing so, view him in many garments. The actor in this case is consciousness. It will be viewed from many perspectives and observed in the context of multiple cultures and schools of thought and belief. If we can get past our conditioning and our habitual thinking about how things "are," we can often see with new eyes, which in turn allows us to envision new possibilities and opportunities.

Through the course of this book, we will dig deeply into the idea of consciousness. We will explore the concept of paradigms as models for organizing, clarifying, and streamlining thinking. We will look at how they have been used and misused, as well as how we might more constructively use them in our lives. We will consider three major trends that are signaling a shift in global human consciousness. Then we will explore several of the mental blueprints from which consciousness operates to transform the things and events we encounter into our experience of life. These include the Seven Levels of Consciousness and three prominent Lines of Consciousness.

We will consider different "paths" across the mental terrain represented by these blueprints. These paths represent different approaches or routes for arriving at our ultimate goal (happiness). We will take a look at some of the promises and pitfalls that each of those paths offers. The aim is to create within ourselves a more informed navigation system (our mind) and thereby improve its ability to reliably take us where we want to go. With a better navigation system, we are much more likely to actually arrive at our desired destination and live happier, more fulfilling lives.

At the end of the book, we will explore certain "mental skills" (the Indices of Consciousness) that drastically improve the mechanical processes of our navigation systems. These skills, when practiced and developed, provide effective and efficient patterns of mental processing that pay big dividends in our efforts to live rich and rewarding lives and to be positive contributors to our communities.

At the end of each chapter, I pose questions around the principles and practice of raising consciousness. These questions serve as focal points for group discussions or individual contemplation. Group discussions can be particularly enlightening, as the astute observer of consciousness has the opportunity to observe consciousness operating in many different variations around a common thought or objective. Moreover, the pool of life experiences of a group is much larger than an individual's and therefore offers a larger "laboratory" within which to observe consciousness in action, or reaction.

The Need for Paradigms

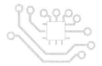

A paradigm is a conceptual model or viewpoint of how things are or work. Throughout history, man has used paradigms to try to explain life and the world around him. As one paradigm—one accepted truth—falls to a newer "truth," mankind evolves. Then a newer viewpoint arises to challenge the old, and the world evolves again. Much like the political landscape, history can be viewed in terms of the rise, collision, and decline of dominant paradigms.

The ancient Egyptians developed elaborate belief systems about life and the afterlife. The Pharaohs were seen as representatives or embodiments of Gods. Enormous pyramids were constructed to house their bodies after death. Extensive measures were undertaken to ensure they had a successful journey to, and comfort in, the afterlife. Servants and huge treasure troves were buried with them, as were detailed instructions for their journey. Their bodies were embalmed to keep them well preserved for future use. Many ancient Egyptians were taught and wholeheartedly believed that the Sun was actually their patron God making his way across the sky each day to survey the world and ensure that all was right. These paradigms gave people a sense of order and predictability in what could be a very harsh and turbulent existence. They provided for many a measure of mental security, peace, and hope. Like the child's monster-zapping box discussed later in this section, these paradigms provided people with a protector that would watch over them and keep their world in order if they lived rightly. The paradigms also provided greater social cohesion through the promise of eternal punishment for those who did evil in society.

In ancient Greece and Rome, extensive and complex mythologies evolved to explain the world. Forces of nature were seen as activities of the gods as they vied for power, cavorted, and unleashed their emotions and will upon the earth. Many held that lightning and thunder were the wrath of Zeus brought on either by men's misdeeds or from frustrations of Zeus's beyond man's comprehension. Aspects of emotion and thought were believed to be the result of direct or indirect influences from the gods, who were believed to have dominion over them.

In the classical age, Greek mathematicians and philosophers such as Pythagoras and Archimedes raised new paradigms for explaining the world based on what they observed, proved, or calculated. The distinction between fact and assumption began to be made. For its clarity and certainty, mathematics was raised to the level of religion in some schools.

Entering the Renaissance, the generally accepted cosmological view was that Earth was the center of the universe, around which the Sun, stars, and planets revolved. Copernicus proposed a totally new paradigm: the Earth revolves around the Sun. This new paradigm was so revolutionary that it shook the established worldview. Because Galileo supported the Copernican view, opposition by those favoring the established paradigm grew more intense. Finally, in the early 1630s, Galileo was tried and convicted of heresy. He carried out the rest of his life under house arrest. Copernicus and Galileo's paradigm, based on what they had observed and believed to be fact, disputed the established paradigm accepted by faith. The benefits of the new paradigm (a more accurate understanding of our reality) conflicted with the benefits of the old paradigm (greater social order). As the significance of the paradigm was fundamental to our understanding of who and what we are, the clash between these two Titans reverberated throughout Europe. But in the end, the paradigm Copernicus birthed and Galileo raised is now accepted as fact.

In the seventeenth century, René Descartes fathered the Cartesian coordinate system and analytical geometry. His new mathematical paradigms explained reality in ways that could be measured, verified, and predicted. Mathematicians could now calculate complex distances, dimensions, and volumes precisely—a feat that would previously have been considered magical or mystical. Descartes also raised the issue of Cartesian dualism, which began an entire branch of enquiry into the nature of the relationship and connection between the mind and the body.

In 1687, fewer than forty years after Descartes' death, Isaac Newton, the father of modern physics, put forth a new paradigm. He asserted that gravity was a natural force, and although it could not be seen, it followed mathematical laws and affected matter. His conceptual and mathematical paradigm for how things work was indeed profound. It gave mankind a depth of understanding about the universe never before achieved. The arbitrary movement of bodies through the heavens now made so much sense that the laws on which they were based could be accurately applied to other systems. A sense of a lifting of the veil from the blueprints of the divine began to emerge. Humanity began to get a fundamental sense of the physical nature of the stage upon which we were acting. Newton's paradigm was so pivotal that it formed the foundation for physics as we know it and went without significant challenge until the arrival of Albert Einstein.

Before even Einstein arrived to shake up Newton's neat, orderly view of the universe we live in, Charles Darwin put forth a new paradigm in his book *The Origin of Species*, which shook our collective identity. It challenged the established paradigm that God created Adam and Eve and all other life in a matter of days. Darwin suggested that creatures evolve over time, dividing into different species and modifying their traits through mutation and natural selection. His paradigm brought forward the picture that humanity was a member of a very large, extended family, whose origins spanned millions of years. Darwin's paradigm fundamentally changed humanity's view of who and what it is, yet it remains controversial in some quarters even today.

And so we see paradigms as they parade through history. They offer an encapsulation of understanding—the best available at the time. Good paradigms benefit us by improving our ability to interact with our world and to live happier, more productive lives. But at best, they state not what is, but rather our best understanding about what is. The distinction is subtle, but an important one we often overlook. Paradigms are made by us, for us. As history has often shown, when we forget this crucial point, we soon find ourselves enslaved by our own creation.

Making Paradigms out of Circumstances

Challenging and difficult circumstances in life are a prime area for paradigm construction and use. Many have felt too often the crushing weight of the loss of a loved one or the tormenting sting of the demise of an intimate relationship. Many have felt the grinding stress of having to endure an unpleasant work environment to feed the family and keep a roof over their heads. Many have wrestled the hissing demons of loneliness, low self-esteem, and depression. Many must contend with death itself in a daily struggle to escape starvation. In still too many parts of the world, the bloody, devastating carnage of war is a daily reality. These parts of life, though common to humanity, grind on us as individuals and tear at our collective souls. Many have said it is not what happens to us, but how we respond to it that really matters. If we can construct and use paradigms that alleviate or even prevent these pains, does it really matter whether the paradigms constitute absolute truth or not? Does it really matter if they're completely "real"?

Long ago, in ancient Sumaria, a man (we'll call him Ivan) worked as an assistant in the king's magician's "science" lab. One day he stole two pieces of a new invention—metal—from the laboratory and took them home. He was impressed with them because they were an "invention." But his wife thought they were ugly and demanded that he get rid of them, so he threw one over the fence into his neighbor's yard to the north and one over the fence into his neighbor's yard to the south.

The neighbor to the north walked out and found the hunk of metal in his yard. He immediately got angry that Ivan had thrown trash into HIS yard. He grabbed the metal, marched over to Ivan's house, threw it on the ground, and proceeded to give Ivan a piece of his mind. From then on, he and Ivan had a tense relationship. The neighbor and his wife even thought about moving out of the area because it had gone so far downhill, having riff-raff like Ivan in it.

The neighbor to the south walked out and saw the hunk of metal in his yard. He noticed it had a sharp edge on it, so he fastened a handle to it and made an axe. With this axe, he cleared his land of trees and became a very prosperous farmer.

Challenging circumstances in life are like that hunk of metal. One man considered it trash, and it ruined his experience and irritated him for years. The other man made it into a tool and improved his life with it. The challenges, difficulties, and pains that we face—do we let them crush us in anger, despair, or grief? Or do we use them to improve our character, strength, and wisdom? We can take the challenging circumstances in our lives and call them trash or call them tools. Either way—trash or tool—in reality, it's just a hunk of metal. We are free to make what we want out of it. Pragmatically speaking, if we see some people turning their "metal" into trash, it drags them down and causes them lots of pain—that's probably not the response we want to use. On the other hand, when we see people making tools and creating real improvements in their lives, their character, or their ability to relate with other people and therefore have better relationships, they have taken the pragmatic view and said, "Let's create tools!" We know it's just a hunk of metal. But we also know we're free to make of it what we will.

Constructively using paradigms is like creating tools. By shaping how we view and what we assume about reality, we can make huge changes in our lives, our societies, and our planet. The fact that people die is like the hunk of metal. Adopting the paradigm that there is life after death creates a tool for many people.

Imagine a global paradigm in which war provided more personal pain than benefit to those in position to start them. Imagine a global paradigm where the loss of any person to starvation was as painful as losing a sibling to the same fate. Imagine a global paradigm where loving every other human being brought an ecstatic exuberance to an individual's experience of life. Such paradigms, when they take hold, change the world. The consciousness revolution is about ferreting out and eliminating the trash we have created that litters our minds. It is also about the realization and use of paradigms, not as truth, but for what they are—tools for interacting with and changing the world. It is about realizing the creative strength that comes from our diversity and using it as an asset rather than grounds for argument. It is about realizing that the divine dwells in all individuals, and if we cannot see it in them, the shortcoming is ours, not theirs.

The urgency for this coming transition is also great. While there are many factors that create war, mass poverty, starvation, deep depression, and other circumstances that crush human life, one thing is clear: our collective thinking and beliefs about these things are a major force of creation and sustenance for these ills. We put a man on the moon. We created the power to exterminate human life on the planet. We are even altering the planet's atmosphere. If we harness the will, surely we can feed the starving. We've ended slavery, why not war? Every day, thousands of people die of causes that could have been easily prevented. Every day, millions of people are wracked with searing emotional pain because they don't know how to effectively process their life circumstances. Are these kinds of suffering and loss of human life things we are willing to accept—or ignore? If so, why?

Suffice it to say that nothing in this book purports to be truth or even an accurate reflection of reality. Rather, it is a proposal in support of the use of various tools for the evolution of human consciousness. It is a proposal for constructing a paradigm we can use to efficiently process the common human experiences in the most beneficial ways we have yet devised.

Paradigms as Tools for the Everyday

Paradigms work on many levels, and not all are so large that they change the world. Some help individuals navigate a frightening world. Take, for example, a young child who is afraid of the dark, trembling in bed for hours fearing monsters in the closet and under her bed. But then the child's father gives her a "magic box" and explains that as long as the box stays on the child's nightstand, it will magically zap and destroy any monsters that come into the room. If the child believes her father, then the box becomes a useful paradigm—the box protects her from monsters. In reality, the box does not destroy monsters. In reality, the monsters don't exist. But if the child is not capable of understanding that the monsters don't exist, belief in the "magic box" paradigm will allow for peaceful sleep.

Paradigms are useful tools in our individual worlds, alleviating our fears and pains and managing our desires. They are the "magic box" to aid us in dealing with life. In the child's world, the protection of the box is real, and it gives her peace and causes no harm. When the child becomes mature enough to understand and believe that the monsters exist only in her mind, the "magic box" paradigm will no longer be necessary. Until that time, the paradigm is very helpful to her. It helps her sleep peacefully and gives her a weapon against fear.

Misinterpretation or Misuse of Paradigms

Sometimes we encounter difficulties when we try to assert our paradigms as "truth" when they have some other use. When I was in the first grade, I took piano lessons. I understood that on paper, the treble clef was a series of lines that ran across the paper and represented intervals in the musical scale. And I also understood that certain notes went on each line, and certain notes went on each space between the lines. But when I first started trying to read music, I had the hardest time remembering which note was supposed to go in which place. Then my piano teacher taught me a very simple saying: "Every good boy does fine." It was a mnemonic device to help me remember which notes went on the lines of the treble clef in ascending order. The first letter of each word stood for a musical note. The notes that went on the lines from bottom to top were E, G, B, D, and F. After learning that phrase, I no longer had trouble determining how the notes were arranged on the treble clef.

Religions, mystical traditions, philosophy, metaphysics, and even physics itself are full of paradigms—simplifications that help us get a better understanding of concepts about God, life, and "reality" much faster. But historically, there has been a tendency for people to latch onto those paradigms and try to make of them unassailable and unquestionable truths. That is like saying the mnemonic I learned in music, "Every good boy does fine," is a recitation of a true statement. It's not—it's nowhere close to it. Its use is in its provision of a structure around which we can learn a difficult task (reading music). Some paradigms are concepts that help us organize our thoughts in a more efficient manner. That, in a more complex way, is the function of a paradigm. Many of the views expressed in this book are just that, paradigms. They are useful ways of viewing the world. Many of the wisest people in history have taught them. Some of these paradigms are seasoned, some are ancient, and some are just now emerging on the scene. But they are not necessarily statements of truth; they are aids to assist us in organizing our thoughts and views in a more efficient and effective manner.

Belief in life after death is a paradigm that has given great comfort to people across many cultures. It made them happier, lessened their fear of death, and lessened their grief at the passing of a loved one. But ultimately, it is a paradigm, and whether it is absolutely true or not cannot presently be proven. And to raise the claim or descend into the debate over whether it is "truth" or "reality" is to create friction and acrimony out of nothing and gain no positive results from doing so. Such has been the bane of religion for thousands of years. Nonetheless, the fact remains that such a paradigm can significantly improve many people's quality of life. Being able to constructively use paradigms while still recognizing they are only paradigms is one of the most useful skills a person can possess. It is one of the hallmarks of an elevated consciousness.

Historically, there has been a trend to get too comfortable in our favorite paradigms. Paradigms are often adopted that work so well for their intended purpose that the paradigm overshadows the principles it was intended to illuminate. The paradigm itself becomes so popular and ingrained that it becomes accepted by many as unquestionable truth. There has always been an element of the human psyche that has sought after and vigorously defended "the truth" or, in other cases, convention. Many in history have demonstrated a willingness, or even eagerness, to fight for and live in "truth" and "reality." However, the wisest of the wise have cautioned us against too strong a reliance on this approach.

○

Real knowledge is to know the extent of one's ignorance.

—Confucius

○

My wisdom is in knowing that I don't know.

—Socrates

○

The way of a fool is right in his own eyes.

—Solomon

○

Questions for Group or Individual Exploration

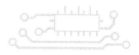

1. What are some examples you can think of that show human consciousness is shifting?

2. What are some examples you know of where people's overfocusing on external circumstances has hindered their own personal growth?

3. How might people's placing their happiness in things over which they have no control be disempowering?

4. In your words, what does raising consciousness mean?

5. In what ways could raising consciousness create a better world?

6. What are some paradigms that have been helpful in your life?

7. What are some paradigms that have hindered you in your life?

8. In your experience, can paradigms be helpful even if they are not literally true?

9. Physics is the scientific study of the laws of nature. In your words, what was Niels Bohr trying to convey by the following statement?

   "It is wrong to think that the task of physics is to find out how nature is. Physics concerns what we can say about nature."[1]

10. In considering the story of Ivan and the hunks of metal:

    a. What are some examples you have observed in which people have made positive use (tools) out of challenges in their lives?

    b. What are some examples you have observed in which people have created negative mountains (trash) out challenges in their lives?

    c. Which approach appears to you to produce better results? Why?

The Convergence of Science and Spirituality

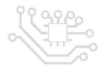

The Power of Uncertainty: The Open Mind

Physicists devote their lives to trying to understand and explain how the universe works. Throughout history, scientists like Galileo and Copernicus have questioned and tested and moved the collective thinking forward. Of course, the work of others has impacted the world as well. I don't mean to diminish the changes wrought by the discoverers of new lands or the philosophers and theologians who challenged the conventional thinking of their day, sometimes at great peril. However, in modern times, it is the physicists whose work has affected us much more than many of us stop to consider.

Einstein's theory of relativity threw a major curve into the straightforward, classical notions of physics set out by Newton. Relativity made strange claims, such as "matter and energy can be converted into each other," and "mass and motion can actually bend time and space." Quantum mechanics (quantum physics) got even stranger as it pried into the workings of the universe at the subatomic level. The tiny "pieces" of the universe, smaller than the atom, exhibited behaviors that appeared bizarre or even impossible under the rules of classical physics. Yet our deciphering of some of the quantum principles has drastically changed how we view our universe and has significantly enhanced our ability to control and modify our environment. The theories of relativity and quantum mechanics have revolutionized the stage upon which humans live their lives. The knowledge that they embody has become integral to much of our everyday experience. The breadth of their reach is staggering—from chemistry to manufacturing to electronics and computers. They are shaping the rules and the means by which we are altering and creating the world around us. Max Tegmark and John Archibald Wheeler state in a February 2001 *Scientific American* article that "an estimated 30 percent of the U.S. gross national product is based on inventions made possible by quantum mechanics, from semiconductors in computer chips to lasers in compact-disc players, magnetic resonance imaging in hospitals, and much more."[2]

Some other technology heavily based on principles of quantum mechanics is laser-powered fiber optics, the centerpiece of the World Wide Web. A world our grandparents couldn't even dream of has emerged as a result. From Facebook to YouTube to Google to modern cell phones, these and many other features of the modern social landscape are outgrowths of that technology.

In 1962, Francis Crick received the Nobel Prize in Medicine for the discovery of DNA. Crick surmised that biology was fundamentally governed by the laws of physics and quantum mechanics. Through Crick's discovery came the eventual decoding of the human genome. The medical possibilities this holds for humanity are mind-boggling. Disease prevention and cure, organ replacement, genetic modification, and even cloning hold incredible promise and possibilities for improving our health and longevity.

Yet, with all of the incredible advances in our understanding of how the universe works, many of the leaders of these advances freely admit they don't truly understand the nature of reality. Perhaps this should give us pause to question our own assumptions about ourselves, other people, and how we think life works. It was these pioneers' openness of mind, their willingness to question what we thought we knew, that opened the door to discoveries that are literally reshaping the world we live in. Here are just a few examples of how different, or even weird, reality can be when compared to what most people think is obvious, and the humility and lack of presumption about how things are that has been displayed by some of our greatest pioneers of understanding.

Alan Lightman defined the theory of relativity as thus:

> Distance and time are not absolute. The ticking rate of a clock depends on the motion of the observer of that clock . . . general relativity proposed that gravity, as well as motion, can affect the intervals of time and of space . . . The gravity of any mass, such as our sun, has the effect of warping the space and time around it.[3]

For most people, the thought that their world and the experiences they have every day are a product of what they think and believe is as odd as the claims of relativity that space and time warp and bend. At first blush, it makes no sense. But when we dig below the surface, the paradigm we uncover holds great power. For so many people, it seems obvious that we have no responsibility for, nor control over, things that happen outside us and our influence. It seems obvious that our misfortunes are the result of external events that crash into us against our will. Yet the less obvious part of the equation is that it is our beliefs and assumptions about those events that determine their emotional impact on us. We may not have control over everything that happens in our lives, but we do have control over what those events mean to us. Consequently, at an energetic and emotional level, our thoughts and beliefs create what we experience from the events that occur. In a fundamental and pervasive way, our minds create our reality. Daniel Styer is the John and Marianne Schiffer Professor of Physics at Oberlin College, and author of *The Strange World of Quantum Mechanics*. Styer describes quantum mechanics and its implications as "weird":

> To our classical sensibilities, the phenomena of quantum mechanics— interference, entanglement, nonlocal correlations, and so forth—seem weird. The various formulations package that weirdness in various ways, but none of them can eliminate it because the weirdness comes from the facts, not the formalism.[4]

Our understanding of quantum mechanics, like relativity, has had a profound impact on our technological and scientific advancement. And yet to attain that understanding, the pioneers of the field had to open their minds to possibilities and realities that were "weird." They had to have the courage and willingness to question convention and, in some cases, toss it out the window completely. After Einstein's development of the theory of relativity turned the world upside down, many scientists and mathematicians began to explore its implications. Quantum mechanics soon arose as an alternate view of how reality works. As understanding along these fronts was pushed further and further into mathematical formulation, even Einstein himself got lost in the wake. Einstein is quoted as saying:

> "Since the mathematicians have invaded the theory of relativity, I do not understand it myself any more."

The irony of Albert Einstein, the father of relativity, saying that he no longer understood the field he singlehandedly created, cannot be overstated. Yet it unveils one of the characteristics of his mind that powered his genius: he had a sense of, and intellectual honesty about, what he did not know. He recognized that a wider reality existed than his mind could comprehend. In pushing forward the forefronts of our understanding of "reality," other great pioneers have exhibited similar humility in the face of deeper understanding.

Werner Heisenberg, one of the foundational contributors to the field of quantum mechanics, admitted to repeatedly asking himself the question: "Can nature possibly be as absurd as it seemed to us in these atomic experiments?" According to Einstein, to be proficient in quantum mechanics—the theory that was reshaping our world—one had to undertake thoughts and notions that might even make the person appear "silly."

○

The more successful the quantum theory is, the sillier it looks.
—Albert Einstein

○

This intellectual courage, a willingness to stand outside the box, resurfaces again and again as a hallmark of innovative genius. It is this childlike openness to new possibilities that empowers us to grow and expand in our thinking and understanding. Another theme that resurfaces over and over is that, paradoxically, it is a willingness to recognize that we don't really understand that often distinguishes those who have the greatest understanding. Richard Feynman received the Nobel Prize in Physics in 1965 for his work in quantum physics. His work included development of a graphic scheme for depicting the mathematical principles explaining the behavior of subatomic particles. These graphic depictions became widely known and used as "Feynman diagrams." As a leader in the field, Feynman said:

I think it is safe to say that no one understands quantum mechanics. Do not keep saying to yourself, if you can possibly avoid it, "But how can it be like that?" because you will get "down the drain," into a blind alley from which nobody has yet escaped. Nobody knows how it can be like that.[5]

Physics and Consciousness

Some of the smartest, most educated, most innovative scientists of our age express bafflement at the "simple" mechanics of the physical world. Perhaps they learned that true wisdom is in knowing we don't really know and that the true nature of reality is beyond our ability to fully comprehend.

Comparatively speaking, the complexity and variables involved multiply exponentially when we move from the mechanics of the "external" world into the realms of the brain and the mind. In terms of complexity, the interaction of subatomic particles is nothing compared to the interactions among people. Thoughts in the brain take place through the transmission of electrochemical signals across the neurons and synapses. It has been estimated that the average human brain has about 100 billion neurons and around 80 trillion synapses. Needless to say, thought is the output of a VERY complex and intricate system of interactions. We really fall off into the twilight zone when we attempt to understand and explain the workings of the human mind as it interacts with others and the world and society around it.

Perhaps it would be prudent to set aside the notion that we really know much of anything. What Niels Bohr, one of the foundational contributors to quantum physics, said about physical nature could also true about our experience of reality: "Everything we call real is made of things that cannot be regarded as real."[6]

The best that we can do is to work with approximations that reflect our current understanding or provide us with happier, more satisfying, and productive lives. And that's what a good paradigm does, even though in reality it is not necessarily "true" or "real." As everything is only an approximation anyway, it would make good sense to use the ones that work the best. This represents the greatest creative union of wisdom and consciousness. In years to come, we will likely have an evolved understanding in which our current paradigms are no longer useful. At that time, we can forge new paradigms that better serve us and reflect a deeper understanding of the universe and ourselves than we are presently capable of. Paradigms are ours for the constructing and ours to use. It seems it would behoove us to create and select the ones that benefit us and put them to work improving our lives and the world.

Synergistic Power:
The Marriage of Intuition and Reason

The primary focus of this book is the power and promise that raising consciousness has for drastically improving individuals' quality of life experiences. In fact, its premise is that raising one's consciousness is the surest means of living a truly happy and fulfilling life. But as will be discussed in more detail, our deep connections to and with each other mean we are not separate, isolated islands of consciousness. Therefore, this book will review the "big picture" of consciousness first, to provide some context within which to view the workings of individual consciousness. This approach will hopefully prove helpful by holding the macrocosm and microcosm of consciousness side by side to illustrate how they reflect each other. As a result, they serve as useful tools, each clarifying the other. Also, in keeping with one of the major themes of this book, I hope to illuminate some of the intimate, working connections between them within the mind.

Back in the days of the cattle drives, a twelve year-old boy bursts into a saloon and shouts, "I'll pay 80 dollars for one of you cowboys to help me with my herd."

One of the cowboys says, "What's the problem with your herd, son?"

The young boy removes his sweat-stained cowboy hat, runs his sleeve across his forehead, and says, "Well, my dad died shortly after I was born. So it's just me and my mom that's running the ranch. And I've gotta drive our cattle up to market in Kansas City all by myself. The problem is, all the Angus cattle wanna go north, and the Brahma cattle wanna go east. And I can't handle 'em all by myself."

"I've got time," says one of the cowboys, "and I could use the 80 dollars. I'll help you."

"Great!" says the young boy. "I'll pay you 20 dollars now and the other 60 dollars when we get 'em to Kansas City. How's that?"

"Fair enough for me," says the cowboy. So the cowboy saddles up his chestnut stallion, swings his spur-spangled boot over the saddle, and follows the boy to the edge of town, where there are 150 cattle slowly walking past main street. The cowboy looks them over and notices they seem very docile and content. "What did you say your problem was, son?"

"All the Angus keep going north, and all the Brahmas keep going east."

The cowboy looks the cattle over and notices they are all Angus. "Son, you don't have any Brahmas."

"Yes I do," says the boy with a puzzled look.

"Ok," says the cowboy, "seeing as how you're young and you didn't have the benefit of a father and all, I'm figuring you don't know a whole lot about cattle."

"I know enough," says the young boy, confidently.

"Well, you don't know what a Brahma looks like, or you'd know you don't have any."

"I know what a Brahma looks like," says the boy indignantly.

The cowboy carefully looks the cattle over once more, making certain that none of them are Brahmas.

"Ok, son. I'll tell you what, if you've got any Brahma cattle, I'll drive 'em to Kansas for free."

"Are you serious?" asks the boy in surprise.

"Dead serious, son. I know a Brahma when I see one, and you don't have any."

"Ok," says the boy. "It's a deal!"

"All right then, show me those Brahmas."

The young boy grins at the cowboy as he turns his horse to the east. "That's what I've been trying to tell you, they're halfway to Waco by now."

The joke, of course, was on the cowboy, but there is a more serious message in the story. Like the two herds of cattle, somewhere in history, science and faith parted company. Each side was like the cowboy acting on what he could see from his perspective but failing to appreciate things outside of it despite the voice of warning. The resulting decisions and courses of action led to misunderstanding within each side's view toward the other. But now we see these camps moving closer to occupying the same terrain, and their hostility toward each other, at least in the Western world, has lessened significantly. From this reconvergence of science and spirituality, a deeper understanding of the human experience is emerging. The first of the three major trends we will consider is reminiscent of the two herds of cattle: the convergence of science and spirituality.

Many esoteric schools of philosophy and mysticism hold that the harmonious union of opposites is a central theme in the process of creation. Through the harmonious blending of two polar opposites, a union is formed from which arises a third, new entity. In biology, we see the principle displayed in the union of male and female and the production of offspring. Many schools of thought view spiritual growth as a process of blending the masculine and feminine energies within our beings.

In the legal profession, we have a long history of the competing views of order and fairness. One view is that rules are inviolate, and offenders should be punished strictly according to the rules so society has certainty upon which it can rely and plan. On the other hand, fairness demands a response that is tailored to the totality of the facts in each individual case. Should a man who steals a car for a joy ride be treated the same as a man who, despite his best efforts, cannot find work and steals a loaf of bread to feed his starving children? The best systems of justice strike a harmonious balance between these two views.

We have observed over millennia the contrasting views between faith and science. One bows its knee to inspiration and unshakeable adherence and the other to reason and proof. And for centuries, there has been a competitive tension between the cultures springing from these two approaches to viewing reality. At various times through the course of history, the tension has held more fangs and claws. But the pressure of the apparent dichotomy, requiring allegiance to one or the other, has been with us. The strident demands of faith during the Inquisition are one example. The dismissive attitudes of scientists toward people of faith as superstitious simpletons is another. The running feud between creationism and evolution theory is a more recent example. But with current advances in science and physics, these two long-competing perspectives are drawing closer to union. While the actual dates of the various components of the Upanishads, ancient Hindu spiritual texts, are debated, many believe their origin to be somewhere around 2,600 years ago. Among some of the ancient teachings of the Upanishads is the concept of the Self, the indescribable Oneness of which we are all expressions:

The flowing river is lost in the sea; the illumined sage is lost in the Self. The flowing river has become the sea; the illumined sage has become the Self.

—Mundaka Upanishad

○

Everything confuses those who regard things as separate from the Self.

—Brihadaranyaka Upanishad

○

Who is this Self on whom we meditate? Is it the Self by which we see, hear, smell, and taste, through which we speak in words? Is Self the mind by which we perceive, direct, understand, know, remember, think, will, desire, and love? These are but servants of the Self, who is pure consciousness. This Self is all in all. He is all the gods, the five elements, earth, air, fire, water, and space; all creatures, great or small, born of eggs, of wombs, of heat, of shoots; horses, cows, elephants, men and women; all beings that walk, all beings that fly, and all that neither walk nor fly. Prajna is pure consciousness, guiding all. The world rests on prajna, and prajna is Brahman.

—Aitareya Upanishad

○

These insightful views came through spiritual sages and their intuitive illuminations. None of their assertions could be proven. Nor could they be disproven. They were assertions of intuitive wisdom, and they had to be ignored, rejected, or accepted as matters of faith.

In her preface to *The Intention Experiment*, Lynne McTaggart summarized some of the astonishing implications coming from the cutting edge of modern physics:

> During my research, I stumbled across a band of frontier scientists who had spent many years reexamining quantum physics and its extraordinary implication. Some had resurrected certain equations regarded as superfluous in standard quantum physics. These equations, which stood for the Zero Point Field, concerned the extraordinary quantum field generated by the endless passing back and forth of energy between all subatomic particles. The existence of the Field implies that all matter in the universe is connected on a subatomic level through a constant dance of quantum energy exchange. Other evidence demonstrated that, on the most basic level, each one of us is also a packet of pulsating energy constantly interacting with this vast energy sea. But the most heretical evidence of all concerned the role of consciousness. The well-designed experiments conducted by these scientists suggested that consciousness is a substance outside the confines of our bodies—a highly ordered energy with the capacity to change physical matter . . . Subatomic matter appeared to be involved in a continual exchange of information, causing continual refinement and subtle alteration. The universe was not a storehouse of static, separate objects, but a single organism of interconnected energy fields in a continuous state of becoming.[7]

The conclusions reached in the Upanishads 2,600 years ago, and the conclusions suggested by scientific research and testing in quantum theory are eerily similar. When we look behind the language and focus on the concepts expressed, it does not take much imagination to see them as one and the same. Intuition and faith, and reason and science appear to be singing the same song.

Moreover, we are seeing an even deeper convergence as they move toward singing in the same key. It would appear that their respective approaches in thought processing are beginning to meld. Historically, scientific conclusions were based on controlled experimentation and mathematical derivations. But with the arrival of the theory of relativity, we saw science begin a turn toward embracing inspiration and faith. Quantum theory pushed that convergence even further.

○

If [quantum theory] is correct, it signifies the end of physics
as a science.

—Albert Einstein

○

Some scientists even claim that string theory is nothing more than mathematical faith, as none of its propositions can be proven or even disproven at this time. The belief that the universe was created by God in seven days has been an article of faith for millions of people. Compare how similar the arguments against intelligent design theory (creationism) and modern string theory have become:

The problem with intelligent-design theory is not that it is false but that it is not falsifiable: Not being susceptible to contradicting evidence, it is not a testable hypothesis. Hence it is not a scientific but a creedal tenet— a matter of faith, unsuited to a public school's science curriculum.[8]

—George F. Will

○

My belief is based on the fact that string theory is the first science in hundreds of years to be pursued in pre-Baconian fashion, without any adequate experimental guidance. It proposes that Nature is the way we would like it to be rather than the way we see it to be; and it is improbable that Nature thinks the same way we do.[9]

—Phil Anderson

○

Superstring theory . . . is, so far as I can see, totally divorced from experiment or observation. . . . there ain't no experiment that could be done nor is there any observation that could be made that would say, "You guys are wrong." The theory is safe, permanently safe. I ask you, is that a theory of physics or a philosophy?[10]

—Sheldon Glashow

○

We are at an interesting juncture in our history when, in many key areas, reason and logic, hampered by our lack of capacity to measure and test, have reached their verifiable limits, at least for now. Some of the experiments required to test some of the modern theories would require a laboratory the size of our solar system.

Paul Dirac shared the Nobel Prize in Physics in 1933 with Erwin Schrodinger for advances in atomic theory and made significant contributions to the fields of quantum mechanics and quantum electrodynamics. Dirac explained how the fundamental mechanics of reality's operation take place beneath the phenomenon of the world as we perceive it and, hence, beyond logic's present capacity to accurately conceptualize it:

> The classical tradition has been to consider the world to be an association of observable objects (particles, fluids, fields, etc.) moving according to definite laws of force, so that one could form a mental picture in space and time of the whole scheme. This led to a physics whose aim was to make assumptions about the mechanism and forces connecting these observable objects in the simplest possible way. It has become increasingly evident in recent times, however, that nature works on a different plan. Her fundamental laws do not govern the world as it appears in our mental picture in any very direct way, but instead they control a substratum of which we cannot form a mental picture without introducing irrelevancies.[11]

For centuries, intuition and reason have battled in people's minds, and in society itself, for supremacy as the primary mode for approaching life. But now we find ourselves in a position where cooperation between the two is the only way forward. Intuition and faith have their weaknesses. Logic has its limits. However, working together, they can enhance each other. At last we are seeing the functional union of reason with intuition, with each supporting and clarifying the other. While this type of consciousness is not unknown in human history, its effective functioning has been the rare exception, found among gifted individuals. Not only does the harmonious, synchronized functioning of the "left-brained" approach with the "right-brained" approach require a certain level of cerebral maturity, the union has also been hampered by the old paradigm of competition: "My view is right and the other views are wrong." As we transition from a paradigm of competition to cooperation, we see the "right versus wrong" view that results from a competitive assumption giving way to the presumption that every view has something to offer. This is having an influence on how we are processing "reality," which is beginning to spread across humanity. Peter Medawar speaks as to how this is becoming normalized processing in scientific thinking:

○

The distinction between—and the formal separateness of—the creative and the critical components of scientific thinking is shown up by logical dissection, but it is far from obvious in practice because the two work in rapid reciprocation of guesswork and checkwork, proposal and disposal, conjecture and refutation.[12]

○

Not only is this union emerging in how we think, but also between cultures and institutions of faith and science. Roy H. Williams believes that string theory "not only reconciles General Relativity to Quantum Mechanics, but it reconciles Science and the Bible as well."[13]

This emerging union is reminiscent of the story of the two blind men who go out for a walk and bump into an elephant. The first man places his hand on the elephant's side and says, "It feels like we've bumped into a wall. This must be a building."

The second man feels the elephant's leg and says, "No it feels like we've bumped into a tree trunk. We must have walked into the woods." And they proceed to argue for fifteen minutes about who's right and who's wrong about what they've encountered.

Finally, a woman walks up and says, "You're both partially right—you've bumped into an elephant, which is both of those things."

As larger and larger segments of society walk away from the paradigm of truth and who's right and who's wrong, they are able to cooperatively pool the "truths" of each perspective and develop a clearer picture of the human experience. Through the course of our history, we have witnessed intuition and faith "seeing" beyond the limits of reason or science. And we have seen reason and science prove some failings in faith and intuition. Today, we are seeing the institutions of science begin to intermingle with institutions of faith and spirituality. And as each comes to respect aspects of the other's view of reality, we are able to arrive at a fuller, clearer picture of the elephant. In the realm of thought, competition is giving way to cooperation. From this monumental union and transformation in the way we collectively process reality, new life is emerging. We are witnessing the birth of a new consciousness across humanity. Even more than witnessing, we are actively participating in the process.

Questions for Group or Individual Exploration

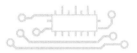

1. If you focus on the commonality of the following quotes, in your own words, what would you say is being described?

   a. "The flowing river is lost in the sea; the illumined sage is lost in the Self. The flowing river has become the sea; the illumined sage has become the Self."

   b. "Everything confuses those who regard things as separate from the Self. Who is this Self on whom we meditate? Is it the Self by which we see, hear, smell, and taste, through which we speak in words? Is Self the mind by which we perceive, direct, understand, know, remember, think, will, desire, and love? These are but servants of the Self, who is pure consciousness. This Self is all in all. He is all the gods, the five elements, earth, air, fire, water, and space; all creatures, great or small, born of eggs, of wombs, of heat, of shoots; horses, cows, elephants, men and women; all beings that walk, all beings that fly, and all that neither walk nor fly. Prajna is pure consciousness, guiding all."

c. "During my research, I stumbled across a band of frontier scientists who had spent many years reexamining quantum physics and its extraordinary implication. Some had resurrected certain equations regarded as superfluous in standard quantum physics. These equations, which stood for the Zero Point Field, concerned the extraordinary quantum field generated by the endless passing back and forth of energy between all subatomic particles. The existence of the Field implies that all matter in the universe is connected on a subatomic level through a constant dance of quantum energy exchange. Other evidence demonstrated that, on the most basic level, each one of us is also a packet of pulsating energy constantly interacting with this vast energy sea. But the most heretical evidence of all concerned the role of consciousness. The well-designed experiments conducted by these scientists suggested that consciousness is a substance outside the confines of our bodies—a highly ordered energy with the capacity to change physical matter. Subatomic matter appeared to be involved in a continual exchange of information, causing continual refinement and subtle alteration. The universe was not a storehouse of static, separate objects, but a single organism of interconnected energy fields in a continuous state of becoming."[14]

2. What are some examples in your life when you have seen an analytical approach conflict/compete with an intuitive approach?

3. When you are confronted with a difficult life decision,

    a. Do you tend to listen to your heart or your head?

    b. What are some ways you might be able to use your heart and your head more effectively together?

4. Considering the story of the blind men and the elephant,

    a. How does its principle relate to how we experience life?

    b. How does its principle relate to the relationship between our experience and interpretation of life and others' experiences and interpretations of life that differ from our own?

5. How might society change if cooperation replaced competition as the prevailing interactive norm?

The Emergence of the Collective Consciousness

The second major trend that is occurring is the emergence of a self-assertive collective consciousness. Many great spiritual teachers have told us for thousands of years that all people are connected to each other. It has been said that the human race, as a whole, has a collective memory of our experiences as a species. But our connection to each other is more than just shared experiences, memories, and cooperation. In some nonphysical way, there appears to be a connection among all people. Spiritual and religious visionaries have seen this connection in spiritual terms, describing it as a common, governing, or guiding spirit. Science has begun to take note of the interconnectedness of reality and is attempting to describe it in mathematical and mechanical terms.

Einstein's theory of relativity illustrated the principle that time and space actually bend and change in response to being interacted with. Modern physics, most especially in the fields of quantum mechanics and string theory, explain that all of reality is merely the interplay of constantly fluctuating energy. Moreover, focused observation or specific awareness of an energetic interaction may inescapably affect that interaction. In essence, consciousness is an integral participant in what otherwise appears to be an external and independent "reality." We now have science pointing to an interconnection between all energy—and energy is the fundamental essence of reality as we perceive it.

An interesting phenomenon often occurs in biology when interconnected components organize themselves into a cooperative network. The second law of thermodynamics states that, in nature, things tend to proceed from a state of order toward a state of chaos. However when "intelligence" is added to the mix, organization and a progression from chaos to order become more probable. Generally speaking, whenever one observes an "environment" proceeding toward greater states of organization and coordinated interaction, intelligence is the driving force. One of the most obvious examples is the evolution of social order that mankind has gone through over the last 10,000 years.

Thousands of years ago, dispersed individuals and small bands of hunter–gatherers first laid the foundation for mankind's ascension to the pinnacle of Earth's food chain. As agriculture developed, larger social organizations, such as cities and city–states, emerged on the scene. When technology advanced, so did the scale and scope of social organizations that humanity experienced. Empires and nations arose. In the present day, multinational political entities such as the European Union are not uncommon. China and India alone represent two examples of billions of people existing together within a distinctly organized social system.

Whenever the members of a defined group in common asso-ciation possess intelligence, the tendency over time is for them to proliferate into ever larger and more intricately interdependent and interconnected networks or organizations. When viewed from the perspective of the network or organization itself, this process can be viewed, metaphorically speaking, as one of "self-development." Take a country as an example of such a social network or organi-zation. Over time, the country tends to develop laws and social customs that reinforce and strengthen it by increasing the coordi-nation, cooperation, and interdependence of its component units, in this case, citizens. To be sure, fractures and fragmentation can and do occur. But by and large, the course in historical terms is clearly toward self-development.

When viewed from a macroscopic perspective, the network itself could be thought of as being intelligent (an "intelligent net-work"). Although that intelligence is originally provided by the "members" the network connects, over a long enough period of time, the intelligence aggregates and becomes self-sustaining on the aggregate level. Typically, the organization itself begins to develop what emerges as its own "culture" or its own "mentality," which is independent of and overarches the individual members of that network. Any citizen with even the most casual observation of government is likely aware of the self-preserving "instinct" that emerges out of governmental bureaucracies. And yet, in historical terms, governments are relatively new creatures. For the broader perspective, we must look to biology.

Every human body begins as a single cell. But that cell grows and divides repeatedly, as do its "offspring." As they grow and multiply, so do the interconnections that support them. A heart and circulatory system become necessary to distribute oxygen and nourishment to each cell. A digestive system becomes necessary to break down food and make it useable by the cells. A respiratory system becomes necessary to supply oxygen to the cells and expel their carbon dioxide waste. A muscular system becomes necessary to enable the body to move and provide for its needs. A network of external senses becomes necessary to enable the body to interact successfully with its environment. All of these systems must be coordinated by yet another system to work in harmony. That is the job of the brain. At last, when a fully developed human body emerges, each and every cell works for the benefit and support of itself and the body as a whole. All of the cells work within the framework of a complex, interconnected system of networks, which is overseen by the brain. In evolutionary terms, while the brain initially emerged as a mechanism for supporting and serving the cellular systems, over time, the brain eclipsed them in importance and power. The brain, as the central coordinator and commander-in-chief of the body's organs and cells, becomes more important than the individual cells it originally merely served. While it is possible to live a full, rich life without an arm, a leg, a lung, or many other large groups of cells, it is impossible to have the experience of life as a human without a brain. In this sense, the brain can be seen as arising out of, but transcending, the cells of the body.

So what began as a simple group of biological units (cells) with extremely limited individual intelligence ends up as an incredibly complex organism or organization of cells. Consequently, we see the principle of self-development at work in biology, just as we see it in sociology. Self-development is a primary characteristic of intelligent networks as we observe them in "physical" reality.

Humans are connected through both physical and extrasensory, nonphysical means. Those connections constitute networks. Because humans—the foundational components that make up those networks—are intelligent, the networks themselves could be considered intelligent networks. As such, they have the trait of being "self-developing."

People have had dreams that have come true. Some people have been visited in their dreams by loved ones at the time of their passing. Many people have had the experience of reading other people's thoughts or feeling their emotions, even though they may be across the state or country. For these people, the extrasensory connections between us are every bit as real as the physical connections. And while our extrasensory connections have remained relatively stable through recorded history, our physical connections have undergone vast evolutions and transformations.

Technology, science, and medicine are enabling us to connect in ways and on a scale never before possible. The line between humans and computers is beginning to blur. Machines are replacing organs in the human body, and companies are field-testing computer chip technologies using biological cells to analyze and store data. The world's information, which functions as our collective memory and ideas, is infinitely more accessible than ever before. The entire Library of Congress can be shot across the world through a fiber optic cable in a matter of seconds. And the information superhighway is ever growing, extending its tendrils in all directions and toward all people. Cell phones connect people through voice and text messaging, transferring information among us at a rate that is super-shrinking the world. This central nervous system is surging with impulses—impulses that relay information that concerns the whole of humanity and that trigger and coordinate collective actions in response to stimuli.

Information freely flows between nations collectively monitoring the potential and actualities of natural disasters. International cooperation has become both commonplace and global in scope. Large multinational corporations span the globe. Our connections to and communications with each other grow ever more pervasive and are moving toward being total and instantaneous. In fact, humanity as a whole is beginning to show intermittent signs of behaving as a single organism.

Billions of people around the world are existing in what was once merely a dream of living in peace with their neighbors, willingly submitting themselves to the rule of law. Millions of people are recognizing that what separates us from each other is infinitely smaller than what joins us. The vision of a family that covers the globe is no longer strange.

Consider a farmer in Idaho who sends food and blankets to displaced refugees in Africa. It makes no sense on an individual level for him to deplete his resources to help someone on the other side of the world, someone whom he has never seen and will never see. But if humanity is viewed as a single organism, it makes perfect sense. As a single organism, it is responding to its own pain. So strong is this tendency that large-scale humanitarian relief efforts involving people from many nations are becoming accepted as a normal part of life on Earth.

With sufficient advancement and development of these physical and nonphysical networks of communication, an organizing intelligence becomes necessary. The overseer and master coordinator that is arising out of our human networks is showing itself as the collective consciousness. In one way of viewing it, the collective consciousness, which is supported by people and the connections between them, is like a giant brain. Conversations, psychic connections, letters, books, radios, phone lines, televisions, e-mails, cell phones, and the Internet—all of the communication connections between humans—can be compared to synapses in the brain. In *Synaptic Self* (2002), Joseph LeDoux explains that "synapses are the main channels of information flow and storage in the brain. Most of what the brain does is accomplished by synaptic transmission between neurons, and by calling upon the information encoded by past transmission across synapses."[15]

As synaptic connections are the "main channels of information flow and storage in the brain," it is clear that a significant increase in synapses produces a significant increase in brainpower. And the power of the collective consciousness is growing exponentially, alongside our channels and flow of communication. The collective consciousness is approaching the developmental stage where it is becoming self-aware. As such, it is beginning to establish its transcendence beyond its individual components (individual people). At the same time, its ability and inclination to advance the welfare of each individual, as well as the whole of humanity, is taking an active leap forward. That is to say, the collective consciousness is self-developing and is becoming both self-aware and self-assertive. In terms of its present developmental stage, it can be thought of as an aggregate intelligence that is just beginning to actively pursue the best interest of "itself," which is humanity as a whole. Increasing cooperation and coordination in global human interaction is one resulting effect through which we can deduce the underlying contribution of the collective consciousness.

Every decade, the signs become clearer that the collective consciousness is beginning to stir. And as the human organism raises itself up and stretches its limbs, it will begin to do something it has never done before: think. Not individually, guided by the thoughts and dreams of particularly enlightened people, but collectively, as the harmoniously joined thoughts of untold numbers of persons, intimately linked by technology and guided by a cooperative spirit.

Questions for Group or Individual Exploration

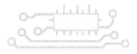

1. How might humanity's increasingly complex and organized social structures over the last 10,000 years reflect an increase in the level of human consciousness?

2. In what ways have you seen people's interconnections grow over your lifetime?

3. In your observations, how would you say this has affected or changed society?

4. What benefits would you say have resulted from these changes?

5. What detriments would you say have resulted from them?

6. Do you think the growth of the United Nations and the formation of the European Union represent a significant trend in the world? Why?

7. In terms of communication, how accessible would you say your circle of friends are to you, compared with how accessible your grandparents' friends were to them? Do you think this has any impact on how we think and behave as a society? How so?

The Critical Value of Expanded Perspectives

𝕿he third trend pointing to the rise in consciousness is the historically unprecedented shift in the conscious perspectives of many people across the globe. The evidence of this is seen in a considerable rise in the individual's ability and inclination to comprehend and address issues, and life in general, from the transcendent perspective of the collective consciousness and the whole of humanity, rather than from his or her personal perspective.

Slavery is one example. From the individualist, self-centered view of the slave owner, slavery is great; it is a free resource from which the owner can benefit and profit. The Code of Hammurabi, which dates from around 1700 B.C., is typical of the ancient view of slavery. It accepted and protected slavery as a valued institution. The Code of Hammurabi states, in part,

> If any one take a male or female slave of the court, or a male or female slave of a freed man, outside the city gates, he shall be put to death.

If any one receive into his house a runaway male or female slave of the court, or of a freedman, and does not bring it out at the public proclamation of the major domus, the master of the house shall be put to death.

If any one find runaway male or female slaves in the open country and bring them to their masters, the master of the slaves shall pay him two shekels of silver.

If the slave will not give the name of the master, the finder shall bring him to the palace; a further investigation must follow, and the slave shall be returned to his master.

If he hold the slaves in his house, and they are caught there, he shall be put to death.

If the slave that he caught run away from him, then shall he swear to the owners of the slave, and he is free of all blame.

This kind of view of slavery was commonplace across the globe. Millions of people were enslaved, deprived, beaten, whipped, raped, starved, had spouses and children taken from them, and were even tortured and killed because others were powerful enough and willing to do it. And while owning slaves was a great boon to he who was in a position to subjugate others, from an objective standpoint, it's a travesty. How many slave owners would have willingly traded places with their slaves? How many had the intellectual capacity and principle to see things from the perspective of the slave? The belief that "I'm not like them" was a too-powerful wall for most to overcome. And yet, in recent history, we have seen the vast majority of humanity not only develop that capacity, but finally act in support of it. This view, this capacity to escape the individual, personal perspective and adopt the perspectives of others, was succinctly stated by Abraham Lincoln: "As I would not be a slave, so I would not be a master. This expresses my idea of democracy."

The perspective expanded, and action followed suit. In the early 1800s, the sentiment against slavery began to formalize. An article by the BBC in review of laws relating to slavery states,

> The modern world accepts that slavery is a great evil and there are many international documents that denounce it and make it illegal. Between 1815 and 1957 around 300 international agreements were implemented, with varying degrees of success, to suppress slavery. Many of these agreements lacked adequate institutions and procedures to ensure that they were enforced. Slavery, slave-related practices, and forced labour are now regarded as:

> - A common international crime when committed against any person.

> - A "crime against humanity" when committed by public officials.

> - A "war-crime" when committed by a nation at war against the citizens of its opponents.[16]

> The "key documents against slavery" listed in the BBC article prove the historical shift in consciousness relating to

the once-accepted practice of slavery:

> The first international document against slavery was the 1815 Declaration Relative to the Universal Abolition of the Slave Trade.

> The Universal Declaration of Human Rights (1948) states, "All human beings are born free and equal in dignity and rights" (Article 1) and, "No one shall be held in slavery or servitude; slavery and the slave trade shall be prohibited in all their forms" (Article 4).[17]

Another example of a shift in the collective consciousness is the decline of tyranny across the globe as democracies and other forms of representative governments have replaced dictatorships. The divine right of kings has given way to the divine right of the people. The law of the jungle has been transformed into the rule of civilized law. And minorities, women, gay people, and the impoverished are taking their rightful place as equals to others. More and more individuals are wielding the power of escaping the restricted, self-centered perspective and are genuinely contemplating the question, "What if I were them?" From that new perspective, they see a wider world, a wider view that informs and changes their attitudes and behaviors toward others. Obviously, these advances are not evenly disbursed across the globe, and they are even largely absent in some countries, but even those countries are making headway. After the historic election of Barack Obama, I heard an interesting interview on National Public Radio. One of the callers, a young black man, was relating a discussion that occurred at his office shortly after the election. He told of standing with two of his friends who were white when an elderly black lady walked up, and with great excitement, said to him: "Isn't this a great victory for us?" He knew by her expression and body language that by "us" she was referring to him, herself, and other black people in the country. The gentleman relayed thinking, *It's not just about us; my two white friends also voted for Barack. It's their victory, too.* The interviewer asked him, "Did you say something to her?" The caller said, "No, being elderly I can imagine what this meant for her, and it wasn't the time or the place to discuss it with her. But I probably will speak to her about it later." Here was a random caller from the public at large, and yet the expanse of his consciousness in that moment was inspiring. He was able to view the situation from his perspective, the perspective of his two white friends, and the perspective of the elderly black woman all at the same time. He had the ability to empathize with what they were likely feeling and to judiciously process all of those perspectives as he was speaking.

This man's fluid capacity to transcend a limited, self-oriented perspective was remarkable. He demonstrated an effective ability to mentally traverse individual, racial, and generational barriers. This level of ability, historically speaking, is remarkable. Yet we are seeing more and more people who are able to process in this way. As a species, our mental agility is significantly increasing.

For the first time in history, humanity as a whole has a real opportunity to entertain such cerebral luxuries. Thanks to the technology and infrastructure we now have in place, a vast number of us have the time, if we so choose to use it, to contemplate perspectives beyond, "How do I survive today and tomorrow?" Moreover, we have greater opportunities and means than ever before to entertain perspectives that differ significantly from our own. Via the Internet, almost every person in developed countries has the opportunity to connect to and dialogue with people from almost every country in the world. A person could easily talk to a diverse group from dozens of countries in a single day if he or she wished. Such access grants us opportunities to explore lives and cultures that are very different from our own. Millions of people are taking the opportunity to do just that. Online communities with members from all over the globe are spreading all across the Internet.

Historically, this is a completely new phenomenon. And yet it opens our eyes to so many possibilities and ways of viewing life. Such connectedness would have been inconceivable 100 years ago. Today, it is a reality for millions of people.

Another significant development is the fluidity with which major segments of the world are able to change perspectives. As democracies proliferate the globe, they bring with them a unique facet: the ability to smoothly and peacefully transform a government and its policies through peaceful elections. Outside of democracies, such changes typically are either violent or accomplished generationally. Many people alive today have witnessed the United States move back and forth between conservative and liberal governments. By historical standards, such sweeping changes are becoming as smooth and fluid as the tide. Through the democratic election process, we are being acclimated to the concept of societal perspective shifts. This has also helped alleviate fear surrounding such shifts, as they typically no longer occur at the risk of life and limb.

Individually and socially, we are seeing a trend toward more fluid perspectives. Such fluidity is a significant sign that consciousness as a whole is evolving. Much like the human body, the maturation process of consciousness can be seen in its increasing coordination and agility. And the more agile it is, the more perspectives it can adopt and consider, and the more situations it can effectively respond to.

Questions for Group or Individual Exploration

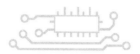

1. How might the historic change in human consciousness regarding slavery serve as an example for all forms of prejudice and injustice?

2. What prejudices or injustices does society presently have that you feel are most detrimental to specific groups of individuals?

3. Assuming you are not a member of one of the groups (being perpetrated against) that you identified in the previous question, if you woke up as a member of that group, how would you want someone in your present position to behave with regard to the discrimination/injustice?

4. Do you feel that people in more affluent nations and neighborhoods have, or should have, any responsibility to the rest of the world? Why?

5. How might democracies be more reflective and supportive of the collective consciousness than dictatorships?

6. How effective are the people in your circle of friends at truly seeing things from others' perspectives?

7. In what kinds of situations are you most likely to try to view things from another person's perspective?

8. In what kinds of situations are you least likely to try to view things from another person's perspective?

9. Why would you say that expanding perspectives might be important?

The Rising Tide
of Consciousness

Why is the course of global consciousness so important to us as individuals in improving our own lives? If we are in fact as connected as the visionaries of science and spirituality tell us, what happens to others is at some level felt by us. If we are all, metaphorically speaking, drops of the same ocean, waves originating even far away will travel to us and move us. Ignoring them will not diminish their action upon us. At levels deep below the conscious awareness of most people, we feel others' pain as if it were our own. For many people, this manifests as a rumbling restlessness with life for no apparent reason. However, there is a very practical reason. The extreme desperation among people in many corners of the globe can quickly spill over and find its way to our doorstep. September 11 demonstrated this. In a rapidly shrinking globe, the dominoes sit close together. Add to that the quickly increasing destructive capacity at our command, and the stakes are rising.

That a revolution in human consciousness is coming seems clear. What is not clear is what ramifications will follow, but lest we be lost in the paralysis of subtlety and indifference, it is worth considering how much just one change in consciousness can accomplish. Consider how much the world changed as mankind modified one of its paradigms—from believing slavery acceptable to considering it unacceptable. Though this change took hundreds of years to accomplish, it had a profound effect on our world and alleviated untold amounts of injustice, misery, and suffering. What was once viewed as a part of life has now been largely transcended and left behind. The predictable results of the primitive law of the jungle's winner-take-all mentality have now been dampened by a change in the way we believe. What more can we achieve? How far can we go? Can war, hunger, and mass poverty be eliminated? Humans are nothing if not creative and resourceful. Perhaps the only real question is when. My question is, "Why not now?"

Jeffrey Sachs, a renowned economist who has worked extensively with developing countries, asserts that for the first time in history, we now have the power to end extreme poverty in the world, if only we can muster the will:

> When the preconditions of basic infrastructure (roads, power, and ports) and human capital (health and education) are in place, markets are powerful engines of development. Without those preconditions, markets can cruelly bypass large parts of the world, leaving them impoverished and suffering without respite. Collective action through effective government provision of health, education, infrastructure, as well as foreign assistance when needed, underpins

economic success. Eighty-five years ago the great British economist John Maynard Keynes pondered the dire circumstances of the Great Depression. From the depths of despair around him, he wrote in 1930 of the Economic Possibilities for Our Grandchildren. At a time of duress and suffering, he envisioned the end of poverty in Great Britain and other industrial countries in his grandchildren's day, toward the end of the twentieth century. Keynes emphasized the dramatic march of science and technology and the ability of advances in technology to underpin continued economic growth at compound interest, enough growth indeed to end the age-old "economic problem" of having enough to eat and enough income to meet other basic needs. Keynes got it just right, of course: extreme poverty no longer exists in today's rich countries, and is disappearing in most of the world's middle-income countries. Today we can invoke the same logic to declare that extreme poverty can be ended not in the time of our grandchildren, but in our time. The wealth of the rich world, the power of today's vast storehouses of knowledge, and the declining fraction of the world that needs help to escape from poverty all make the end of poverty a realistic possibility by the year 2025.[18]

In the preface to his book, Dr. Sachs points out how this transformation would come about: "When the end of poverty arrives, as it can and should in our own generation, it will be citizens in a million communities in rich and poor countries alike, rather than a handful of political leaders, who will have turned the tide."[19] While it might be easy to dismiss his assertions as unbridled optimism, let's take a look at some of the facts on the ground. According to World-watch Institute's estimates, here's what it would cost to provide

Universal literacy:
$5 billion.

Clean drinking water for all:
$10 billion.

Reproductive health care for all women:
$12 billion.

Elimination of hunger and malnutrition:
$19 billion.[20]

If we doubt the power of the people or the resources at our disposal, here are some eye-opening statistics of actual annual global expenditure figures from Worldwatch:

Makeup:
$18 billion.

Ice cream in Europe:
$11 billion.

Perfumes:
$15 billion.

Ocean cruises:
$14 billion.

Pet food in Europe and United States:
$17 billion.[21]

Just as with slavery, what if humanity as a whole changed its paradigm from "extreme poverty and deprivation are a part of life on earth" to "extreme poverty and deprivation are unacceptable"? It will not be the machinations of governments or wealthy philanthropists that carry the day, it will be a revolution in global consciousness spread across millions of its citizens. This revolution in consciousness will recognize our Oneness to a degree never before realized on a mass scale. It will be a consciousness of love that counts every human being as a member of the family, a consciousness that is cognizant of those outside our daily experience, and a consciousness that daily asks the question, "What if I were them?" It will be a consciousness where more and more of us come to a realization of that profoundest of paradigms: "They ARE me."

Some interesting research and conclusions are emerging from the study of thought and intention. While the mystics have proclaimed for ages that our thoughts influence the world around us, recent scientific experiments are shedding light on how. In *The Intention Experiment*, Lynne McTaggart summarizes some of the findings coming out of experiments in this field. (Gary Schwartz has done extensive scientific research into the connections between psychic healing and electrical and magnetic fields.)

Gary Schwartz's creative experiments revealed to me something fundamental about the quantum nature of thoughts and intentions. He and his colleagues had uncovered evidence that human beings are both receivers and transmitters of quantum signals. Directed intention appears to manifest itself as both electrical and magnetic energy and to produce an ordered stream of photons, visible and measurable by sensitive equipment.[22]

The revelation that thoughts actually emit electromagnetic energy becomes even more intriguing in light of some of the other discoveries. "Intention appears to be something akin to a tuning fork, causing the tuning forks of other things in the universe to resonate at the same frequency."[23]

This phenomenon of entrainment suggests that thought and intention tend to produce an organizing and harmonizing effect on their environment. Indeed, this facet is consistent with the observation that where intelligence is involved, the environment tends to proceed from chaos to a greater state of organization and harmony. This occurs despite the second law of thermodynamics's expectation of a progression from order to chaos. McTaggart goes on to state, "A body of research also suggests that the power of an intention multiplies, depending upon how many people are thinking the same thought at the same time."[24]

This principle highlights the significant fact that there is a synergistic strength in numbers. The more people become aligned with an intention, the greater the influence it has on their environment. And perhaps most astounding is that it has a like effect on other people:

In earlier work, Grinberrg-Zylberbaum had discovered that brain-wave synchrony occurred not only between two people, but between both hemispheres of the brains of both participants, with one important distinction: the participant with the most cohesive quantum wave patterns sometimes set the tempo and tended to influence the other. The most ordered brain pattern often prevailed.[25]

This evidence highlights the concept of entrainment, where the most-ordered brain pattern influenced less-ordered brain patterns into greater order. In her review of extensive research of people who were accomplished healers, McTaggart covers some interesting findings on thought: "Schwartz now had his answer about the nature of conscious thought: healing intention creates waves of light—and indeed these are among the most organized light waves found in nature."[26]

Harry Edwards is one of the most notable and studied healers of the modern day. His dedication to spiritual healing and the studies of his work have been credited by some as playing a major role in the acceptance of registered healers treating their patients in hospitals.

> To Edwards, the most important act [in healing] was moving aside, shedding the personal ego, making a conscious attempt to get out of the way. Cooperstein's healers described their experience as a sense of total surrender to a higher being or even to the process. All believed that they were part of a larger whole. To gain access to the cosmic, nonlocal entity of true consciousness, they had to set aside the limiting boundaries of the self and personal identity, and merge with the higher entity.[27]

It appears that it is the unselfish and egoless desire of the healers to help that either creates or enables the healing power to function through them. These qualities—unselfishness and a desire to help—are cornerstones of what we call "love." Such research is casting new light on the profoundness of the assertion that love conquers all. In terms of thought patterns, this appears to be the case. The research also points to the usefulness of the ancient paradigm of the mystics of old: we are all one. Such sentiment was also reflected by one of the greatest minds of human history:

○

A human being is part of the whole, called by us "universe," a part limited in time and space. He experiences himself, his thoughts and feelings as something separated from the rest—a kind of optical delusion of his consciousness.

—Albert Einstein

○

Such a view is extremely powerful and holds great promise for the healing and nurturing of humanity. From this, we can devise the emergence of a new paradigm, one of humanity as a single organism, where every human is a member of our family. Indeed, many sages have asserted that this is the key to our evolutionary future. Imagine the possibilities where cooperation rather than competition is the prevailing sentiment across humanity. If a critical mass of people can live in this perspective, the majority of humanity will be entrained to this attitude as well.

In many ways, religion and science have pointed to the same fundamental conclusion: beyond the individual is a source of greater intelligence and power. Yet they have come to this conclusion from vastly different perspectives. As has previously been stated, at times those diverse perspectives have been quite hostile toward each other. Rather than work on developing understanding within the common ground upon which they agree, countless energy and lives have been lost in fighting over who's right and who's wrong.

Many of the old paradigms upon which humanity has operated have held fatal limitations. These limitations often wreaked havoc and destruction across the globe. While millions of people believed their view to be "the truth" or "the right one," many of the great minds of our history have proclaimed the fallaciousness and counterproductivity of this view. It entrenches people in separate camps, advocating for their favorite perspective of reality. Imagine for a moment that humanity walked away from its futile quest to hold and propagate "the truth." Imagine instead that we operated from a shared paradigm—not because it was "right" or "the truth," but because it was proven to be a useful tool for benefiting individuals and humanity. The beauty of using the collective consciousness as a paradigm for explaining human evolution is its utility as a commonly acceptable model. While it recognizes a higher intelligence, that view is seen as a paradigm created by us to benefit us, and it is subject to improvement as our understanding evolves. Research and discussion can be exchanged on overarching patterns in human life that appear to be influenced or directed by an intelligence extending beyond any individual's without having to broach the subjects of the existence or nature of God. The presumption of a collective consciousness is completely independent of the question of the existence or nonexistence of God and is compatible with either view. The devout believer and the atheist can hold a civil dialogue without assumptions of faith erecting an impenetrable barrier. No argument need be had on whether the paradigm is true or not, only on whether it is a useful model in light of our research, information, and life experiences. Science and religion could set aside their differences and work cooperatively on common ground to pursue an understanding of consciousness and intelligence that includes and transcends individuals. Moreover, the collective consciousness as a paradigm holds no cultural affiliations or biases. Indeed, its characteristics have shown themselves in all ages and all cultures in all corners of the globe.

Proceeding with a paradigm based on a collective consciousness could provide a framework for unclogging a major ideological logjam and also provide a structure for organizing and streamlining other paradigms. And while it might be easy to get lost in the scope and scale of such undertakings, fortunately luck is on our side. As fate would have it, while elevating global consciousness is critically important to the welfare of humanity as a whole, it is also the most beneficial pursuit individuals can engage in for themselves. As we survey the paradigms most useful for humanity, they show themselves to be the same paradigms that are most useful for us as individuals.

Questions for Group or Individual Exploration

1. How realistic do you think the goals of ending war, starvation, and extreme poverty worldwide are? Why? What do you see as the biggest obstacles to achieving those goals?

2. How might the world change if the vast majority of people believed that all other people were extensions of themselves?

3. What ramifications could you see if you were to assume that, at an energetic level, minds with more cohesive (harmonious) wave patterns tend to influence minds with less cohesive brain patterns?

4. Why might making a conscious attempt to get their ego out of the way be helpful to spiritual healers when they are attempting to help others?

5. How might a widely acceptable paradigm be useful in bringing people together?

6. Why might the consciousness paradigm be useful as a common model for discussing life experiences?

7. What might be some of the weaknesses and limitations of using the consciousness paradigm as a common model for discussing life experiences?

The Mind as a Machine in Pursuit of Joy and Satisfaction

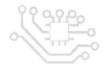

Having begun at the outside and worked inward, let's now reverse the mirror and examine paradigms from the inside working out. What each of us as individuals wants is to be happy. Indeed, that is the great preoccupation of life: increasing our happiness. How best to achieve that is the $64,000 question. While certainly everyone is an individual, there have proven to be some paradigms that are generally useful across broad ranges of individuals. One common theme is the importance of realizing and living life to the fullness of who we are.

Who wouldn't want to live an amazing life, be wealthier than we can imagine, live in a vibrant and fulfilling romantic relationship with our soul mate, and have an extensive list of loving and supportive friends? Who wouldn't want to be admired and respected, successful beyond our expectations, and leave a lasting, meaningful legacy of contribution to the world? That's the stuff of dreams and legends. So few actually get to have these experiences, and yet they are available to anyone who truly wants them. But to achieve them, we have to quit chasing them with our "smaller mind" and use our "greater mind." Our failings are not failures in achievement, but failures to live in our full potential. The greater mind can easily accomplish feats that would crush the smaller mind. Most people live their entire lives as only a fraction of who they truly are. When we realize the fullness of who and what we are and live in our full potential then dreams routinely come true. More to the point, they foreshadow the reality that is to come.

Long ago, the Oracle of Delphi proclaimed, "There is none wiser than Socrates." And Socrates's greatest admonition to us was "Know thyself." The vast majority of humanity is trapped within an extremely contracted view of who and what one is. Spiritual visionaries through the ages have made this observation. Central themes of their teachings promote that we are far more powerful and divine than we can imagine. When people's consciousness evolves such that they come to a realization of their true selves, they undergo an amazing transformation in being. When Buddha attained enlightenment, he obtained an incredible spiritual wisdom and power so profound that it totally changed him. When asked about his transformation, he compared it to having been asleep all his life and then waking up. Thereafter, he operated in the profoundest reaches of wisdom and had continuous access to Nirvana. Take a moment and consider the difference in your experience of life between when you're asleep and when you're awake. Clearly, Buddha was pointing to a profound transformation.

Jesus described this transformation as being akin to the physical person's dying and then being reborn as both a physical and

spiritual being who may obtain entrance into heaven. The transformation he spoke of was a total transformation, empowering the
individual in a way he or she had never known previously. If we
can attain this transformation in consciousness, we will begin to
live life through the greater mind. Challenges that we would have
previously been stupefied and overrun by simply evaporate before
us. Our capacity to perceive and effectively respond to the circumstances and opportunities in our lives is multiplied.

There can be little doubt that the most powerful things we have
are our minds. It is the human mind that secured our reign at the
top of the food chain. It is the mind that has created much of the
physical world we experience. It is the human mind that created
wonderful works of art and literature and incredible innovations in
medicine, science, and technology. The human mind is so powerful
that it has even changed the face of the Earth. And it is our minds
that shape who we are, the actions we take, and our daily experience of reality. Whether it is the choices we make or the beliefs we
hold, our minds to a large extent determine what our lives will be.
Even if we avoid decisions, that is a decision in itself. Seeing that
the mind is the most powerful machine we possess, it makes sense
to devote great care and effort in tuning and honing its operation.
It is by liberating ourselves from the smaller mind and graduating
to our greater minds that we supercharge our lives.

Through transforming our minds, we gain two major benefits:
greatly increased wisdom and enhanced personal power. What the
fool does in a hundred steps the wise man does in one. Wisdom
provides us greater effectiveness and efficiency and enables us to
accomplish more with much less effort. Additionally, it greatly

enhances our personal power as our motivation and enthusiasm rise markedly. These changes enable us to live in harmony with our higher goals and aspirations. When we increase both power and efficiency, we get a dramatic increase in productive output. While the quantity of our output may increase, the primary improvement is in quality. Moreover, all the additional output can be applied directly to achieving our dreams.

Raising our consciousness is not a goal to be attained; it is a way of living life. It is the beliefs, attitudes, and practices we employ every day that carry us to fulfillment. Transforming consciousness is not a destination to be arrived at; instead, we should consider living life as an exciting journey filled with surprises and wonderful experiences. If the mental machinery is well tuned, its mere operation produces joy and fulfillment.

The work of breaking free of our smaller minds takes time, but with every established improvement in mind functioning, we get a boost that pays dividends every day thereafter. And fortunately, the benefits are cumulative. But this path is not for the timid or weak of heart. Sadly, countless people would prefer to stay in unhappy circumstances and complain about them rather than undergo the discomfort of changing themselves. Many turn back because it is too uncomfortable to face certain things about themselves or their beliefs. So instead of pushing forward, confronting their demons, and making the necessary changes to overcome them, they carry on in denial. Although perhaps easier in the short run, this course seals their fate in circumstances they don't like. All true changes in our world must begin within ourselves. The world we perceive is largely a reflection of what we think and believe, and the surest way to change our world is to change our minds.

There can be no doubt that changing ourselves is hard work. It takes effort to change habits and ingrained beliefs. As Lao Tzu said, "He who overcomes others is strong, but he who overcomes himself is mighty." We can realize our dreams, but we must be mighty. We must have the courage and determination to push ourselves out of our comfort zones and venture into the unknown. We must try things we have never tried before. We must be willing to abandon beliefs that do not serve us. While we can realize our dreams—and this book can suggest one path for doing that—if you are unwilling to change yourself, nothing that can be said will help. The only one who can truly effect change in a person is that person. Only he or she has the power to liberate himself or herself from a smaller mind. As the saying goes, "If we keep doing what we've always done, we'll keep getting what we've always gotten." Albert Einstein is credited with saying, "Insanity is doing the same thing over and over again and expecting a different result." The nature of life is to adapt (change) and grow. In a sense, if we aren't adapting and growing, we're slowly dying.

Many have asked, "How long does it take to transform one's consciousness?" Every individual is different, but rest assured that it typically does not happen overnight. It requires a long-term commitment. Research shows that, on average, it takes thirty days of consistent effort to change an ingrained habit. Entrenched belief systems that have been built up over a lifetime can take significantly longer to deconstruct and let go of. Some people take ten years or more of hard work to achieve a Level of Consciousness with which they are satisfied. Others achieve it in significantly less time. But if people earnestly apply themselves and diligently make the necessary changes within themselves, in one year they should have enough experiences to recognize that they truly do have the power to drastically transform themselves and their lives.

The counterintuitive premise that we can only truly change our world by changing ourselves seems strange at first. Accepting full responsibility for our life's not being everything we want it to be can be a bitter pill to swallow. But we must if we are to improve our lives. And while the prospect of having to completely change how we think and what we believe in order to realize our dreams is daunting, even frightening, there is good news. While there are some things in our lives that are easier to change than ourselves, we are the one thing we have the full, unobstructed power to change. Although the full responsibility to change lies squarely on our shoulders, so does the power. Fortunately, they go hand in hand.

The process of change and growth is often like a seesaw. We boldly launch into a new approach or modify a belief, but then we retreat back to the comfort of the old way . . . and the negative conse- quences it brought. Then we try the new way again and retreat again, back and forth, until we are convinced the new way is better. This is a natural process, but it also slows our evolution in direct propor- tion to the amount of time we spend teetering back and forth. Those who are committed to living life at higher levels of consciousness must make peace with the fact that change will be uncomfortable. And they must accept and embrace this price as part of the process. An additional factor that must be expected is that relationships will change. The person who is committed to living life at a higher Level of Consciousness might leave some friends and family behind. Change is uncomfortable because there is typically a large degree of doubt or fear. And our changes will likely raise these feelings in others who do not understand what we are doing. Our changes can cause them to doubt themselves, and they may attempt to ease their discomfort by trying to suppress our changes. But we must press on, as it is our responsibility as human beings to live as our authentic selves. Any relationship that would intentionally thwart us from that is probably better left behind. If we tell others about our changes, we should be prepared to face discomfort in some of those people.

What has the process of elevating consciousness done for people? It has removed and cured people of deep depression, reduced stress and anxiety, increased joy, transformed unhappy relationships into blissfully romantic and emotionally fulfilling relationships, markedly increased career success, triggered spiritual revelations, enabled people to determine their life's purpose, overcome poor self-esteem, unlocked and enhanced psychic abilities, reformed judgmentalism, fostered compassion, created an abundance of loving relationships, brought abundance to people's lives, broken down walls of isolation and loneliness, enabled a direct perception of the divine, eliminated prejudice, enabled unconditional love, fueled philanthropic endeavors, enhanced wisdom, and conquered fear, among many other things. How can one process—the process of elevating consciousness—affect so many areas of life? The mind is the machine through which all these things are created and/or experienced. Improve the machine, and all of its output is improved.

Consider the attitudes of Ted and James in the following example:

Susan was a student in college. On her way to class one day, she saw her friend Ted. Ted appeared to be rather perturbed, so Susan asked, "Hey, Ted. What's wrong?"

Ted said, "I'm having a crappy week. I was in a car wreck yesterday. My car got smashed up, and it's in the shop. So I'm going to be without a ride all week; it's going to cost $600 to fix it, and I'm really not happy about it."

"I'm sorry to hear that, Ted." said Susan. "I hope your week gets better."

"Me too. It couldn't get much worse," said Ted as he walked off.

Three minutes later, Susan bumped into another friend of hers. "Hey, James, how are you?"

"I'm doing great!" said James. "I'm really lucky. I was in a wreck yesterday and nobody got hurt—I'm not even sore!"

Ted and James had the exact same experience. Ted emerged from it feeling greatly inconvenienced, oppressed, and upset. But James emerged from it feeling fortunate. Although they had the same experience, their perception of the quality of their lives at that time was quite different. While it's impossible to say one view was right and the other was wrong, we can say with certainty that Ted's view of the event made him much less happy. Ted gained no benefits over James by holding the negative view he did, and if quality of life is measured in terms of happiness, James's view of the event did provide significant benefits over Ted's view.

This is one simple example of how changing the way our minds process information can enhance the quality of our lives. As our consciousness evolves, we come to realize that many assumptions we make about life have similar ramifications. Often, the assumptions are more subtle and seemingly less connected to our experience of life, yet their effects may be far greater. Here are a few examples: whether people are inherently good or bad, how we should respond to fear, how personal worth ought to be measured, what motives we assume people are acting from, how right and wrong should be determined, how we should respond to injustices, the role of forgiveness, what kind of creatures we are, whether there is a higher power, and whether the higher power judges us, loves us, or is indifferent to us. While these assumptions may seem remote from our day-to-day experience, they typically carry a greater impact because they relate to many of our experiences, albeit in a much less obvious way.

One of the goals of elevating consciousness is to bring these subtle assumptions and their interconnections to the surface and to analyze their utility. Do they make us happier and enrich our lives, or do they bring us down and hamper our ability to positively and enjoyably relate to others? Do they empower us to live the kind of life we want, or do they sap our strength and creativity?

Questions for Group or Individual Exploration

1. What are some things in life a person might want more than he or she wants happiness?

2. Would not having those things make the person significantly less happy?

3. Explain the following statement: "Raising consciousness is not a goal to be attained; it is a way of living life."

4. How would you compare the "smaller mind" with the "greater mind"?

5. What examples have you observed in which people have refused to make changes within themselves that would likely have improved their lives? Why do you think they behaved in this way?

6. How do making excuses and blaming others for things we don't like disempower us?

7. What are some of the reasons why change and growth are frequently so uncomfortable for people?

8. What are some examples of ways in which our fundamental beliefs about God, fate, good and evil, and the nature of people influence how we interpret—and thus experience—some of the daily events in our lives?

The Power of Higher Consciousness

So what is this awakening, this rebirth that opens us up to the fullness of our selves? In simple terms, it is transcending our physical, body/brain perspective of reality and adopting a holistic perspective. Many people refer to this as transcending the ego. But "ego" is a bit confusing, as the operative definitions of ego can be quite varied. Many people think of the ego as the seat of self-centeredness, pride, and greed. But it is more than that. It is also the mental construct that causes us to experience reality as an individual, separate and distinct from others. It is the ego that draws the line where "I" ends. It is the ego that recognizes us as a physical body and tells us that "we" end at the surface of our skin. The job of the ego is to drive us to secure our bodily needs and safety. It is the ego that also serves as lookout for potential threats and sounds the alarm that throws us into fight-or-flight mode. The ego is essentially the alarm system for the vehicle (our body) that we drive. While the ego has been an essential element of our psyche that has ensured the survival of our species, its rulership of our psyche in the modern age is problematic. Relative to our historical experience as a species, few people are at risk of winding up as an animal's meal. And peace is presently prevalent across most of the globe. But the body's guardian, the ego that protected us during life in the jungle, remains in a suspect position of authority for most of us. The times have changed, and with them we have the luxury of transferring power from our smaller minds (the ego) to our greater minds. Our greater minds are not ruled by the law of the jungle, but rather by the law of love.

Mahatma Gandhi, known as the tiny brown man in the loin-cloth, wielded extraordinary power. He led India in a historically unprecedented bid for independence from Britain. He successfully secured impoverished India's independence from a wealthy nation with global military might. Now that was amazing power! Moreover, he did it with total nonviolence—a miraculous accomplishment. Gandhi was able to achieve this because he lived from his greater mind. And one of the admonitions that Gandhi repeatedly gave to those he spoke with was this: "We must transcend the ego." Gandhi well understood that it is the ego that keeps us asleep, unborn to our greater minds. But the ego is a jealous ruler and will fight us tooth and nail if we try to replace its historical position on the throne. It will use any trick at its disposal—doubt, fear, confusion, even agony—to avoid having to give up the throne to the greater mind. But if we wish to elevate our consciousness and transform our lives and the world, we must make this transition. Gandhi did, and look what he accomplished.

Not many years ago, a spiritual sage spoke to his friends about the ego. Many of them had been wrestling with the concept in their efforts to transcend their egos and live from their greater minds. He used a metaphor through which to view the bigger picture. He walked with them out into the woods and gathered them beneath a large oak tree. As they sat on the ground among its sprawling, running roots, he said,

> The divine is like a mighty, sacred oak . . . and it drops its seeds as acorns. Every human being is an acorn. We fall to Earth and land upon its soil. From there, we look around and see an endless field of acorns. Tiny seeds that are encased in a protective shell we call the ego. And we are vulnerable, hiding from the birds and squirrels that would eat us. For thousands and thousands of years, we've hidden, but we've climbed to the top of the food chain. And where do we go from here? Some acorns live in fear—fear of the birds and squirrels that would eat them—and they hide within the safety of their shell. But other acorns look up at the divine oak and say, "Why am I not like that?" And for them, the ego—the shell that surrounds the acorn and protects it—becomes a prison. A few acorns split through their shells and send tiny roots down into Mother Earth; they send shoots up into Father Sky. And then they begin the process of real growth. The turning point for every acorn is breaking through the ego shell, exposing itself, and allowing itself to grow. Within every acorn that will grow dwells the mighty oak.

> And you have taken the bold and courageous step of cracking your shell and exposing yourself. You have had the audacity

to crack the ego and be who you truly are. You've taken on the vulnerability and uncertainty that comes with growth. For this courage, you are on your way to becoming mighty oaks. I'm here to tell you that we are at the dawn of a new era. For thousands of years, humanity has seen itself as the acorn. But more and more, the vision of the divine, mighty oak is catching hold. And the chosen ones are waking up and looking around. And they see around them not what is, but what will be: a vast multitude of oaks separated from this reality only by their tiny shells and time. Because you've had the courage to be your true self, you've been offered the gift of that vision. It is your soul, your higher self, that directs your transformation from the acorn to the oak. This miraculous power comes from within you. This secret, on some level, you know. And so you've allowed the vulnerability and pain that comes when the soul breaks through the ego and begins its journey of growth with tender, vulnerable shoots.

You are the first of many saplings in the coming sacred grove of oaks. You are midwives to the offspring of the divine. And how do you, as midwives, usher in the sacred grove? Join hands with Father Sky and Mother Earth, and with your brothers and sisters—the saplings and those who still live as acorns—and nourish your brethren. Feed them with the light of the fire from your soul's deepest passion, and water them with your love. Dig deep and dream boldly, and become what you dream. See the divine in all things. Be the oak that you are so that others can see what awaits them. I tell you now, that you are the cocreators of Heaven.

And the time for this is now. Countless lives have waited and labored in their sleep to bring you to where you are. Carry on with courage and faith and love, and till the soil for others to grow from. Consciousness is the last great frontier for us. It is the soil from which this sacred grove will arise. Take this gift and use it. Flourish with it and in it. Become the fullness of the giant oaks you are. For the path to the mighty, sacred grove runs through you.

The story of the oaks represents the paradigm shift we are presently faced with: from viewing ourselves as acorns to viewing ourselves as oaks. We must start using the measuring stick of the soul rather than the measuring stick of the ego. By elevating our consciousness, we make this transition from our smaller mind to our greater mind. And as we do so, we achieve a higher order to our thoughts. Fortunately, raising consciousness is not an inborn talent, it is a skill that everyone can learn. It could be thought of as the skill of organizing and effectively using the mind. Research has indicated that people's focused thoughts seem to exhibit the property of influencing others' thoughts to come in alignment with theirs. Research has also indicated that those who have practiced "boosting their signal" by increasing the coherence of their thoughts exert greater influence than those who have not.

But how exactly do we raise our consciousness? How do we achieve the greater mind? As has already been alluded to, healing intention arising from unselfish love appears to produce some of the most well-ordered light that has been found. By transcending the limiting confines of a physical identity and the smaller mind/ego that governs it, a wider world opens. The fact that selfless love is a central key comes as no surprise to anyone. That claim has been made by many voices across many cultures and ages. But what was once an article of faith is now garnering the support of scientific evidence. In her review of research on remote influence, McTaggart points to the implication that selflessness expands a person's power to interact with and influence his or her environment in a manner outside traditional physical or communicative influence:

> In Krippner's experience, certain personalities are more susceptible to merging identities than others: those who, according to a psychological test, possess "thin boundaries." According to the Hartmann Boundar Questionnaire test, developed by Tufts University psychiatrist Ernest Hartmann to test a person's psychological armament, people with thick boundaries are well organized, dependable, defensive, and as Hartmann himself liked to put it, "well armored," with a sturdy sense of self that remains locked around them like a chain-link fence. People with "thin" boundaries tend to be open, unguarded, and undefended. Sensitive, vulnerable, and creative, they tend to get involved quickly in relationships, experience altered states, and easily flit between fantasy and reality. Sometimes, they are not sure which state they are in. They do not repress uncomfortable thoughts or separate feelings from thoughts. They tend to be more comfortable than thick-boundaried people with the use of intention to control or change things around them. In a study by Marilyn Schlitz of musicians and artists, for instance, creative individuals with thin boundaries also scored best in remote influence.[28]

The evidence indicates that those who are able to transcend their egos have a higher probability of remote influence, presumably by attaining higher-order thought patterns. This proposition is in line with common sense, which would tell us that a person who can entertain multiple points of view is exercising a stronger mental muscle than the person who can only operate from one. Quite simply, the greater mind operates on a broader range of views than does the smaller mind.

This is a major facet to the evolution of consciousness, recognizing, "It's not just about me." Once again, we see evidence coming in to support the paradigm that we are all connected and, in that sense, one. The more we can live in that paradigm, the more ordered our thoughts become and the more we are inclined to value other people. This can be stated in the principle that the higher the order of our thinking, the broader the scope of beings we identify with; thus, higher-order thoughts bring broader identifications.

Another key aspect of elevating our consciousness is the increase in power we receive from it. Returning to the nature of thought and intention, McTaggart discusses the results of a series of tests run by Schwartz and Melinda Connor, a colleague of Schwartz and a postgraduate fellow with an interest in healing. Connor approached Schwartz, proposing some tests to measure magnetic fields emanating from the hands of Reiki practitioners and other master healers with track records of successful, dramatic healings. These tests indicated that significant surges in electromagnetic energy came from these healers' hands when they were engaged in healing. McTaggart connects the fluctuations in energy coming from their hands to the healers' states of mind thusly: "Schwartz and Connor had their proof that directed intention manifests itself as both electrostatic and magnetic energy."[29]

Electromagnetic energy can be thought of in one sense as waves of energy. Light is a well-known electromagnetic energy. Let's take a brief look at some of the evolution of scientific thought in this area.

Isaac Newton
January 4, 1643–March 31, 1727

Isaac Newton is considered the father of modern physics. He ushered in a revolution in human understanding with his theory of gravity, which states that mass exerts an attractive force on mass. This force acts across empty space, and larger masses (like planets and stars) exert proportionally larger forces that act over greater distances than smaller masses.

Michael Faraday
September 22, 1791–August 25, 1867

Michael Faraday was focal in his development of our understanding and use of electricity. He demonstrated that an electric field exerts a force on electrically charged objects. This field can penetrate both empty space and matter. He also formulated the magnetic field concept. His experiments showed that a magnetic field can affect light as it travels.

James Clerk Maxwell
June 13, 1831–November 5, 1879

James Maxwell solidified our understanding of the interrelationships between numerous physical phenomena that had previously been viewed as unrelated to each other. He is considered the father of electromagnetic theory. Maxwell showed that electric and magnetic fields form waves that travel through space. He also demonstrated mathematically that electrical and magnetic forces and fields were interrelated. The formulas that describe these interrelationships are known as "Maxwell's equations." Maxwell was also the first to propose that light was, in fact, an electromagnetic phenomenon.

Albert Einstein
March 14, 1879–April 18, 1955

Albert Einstein introduced a number of revolutionary concepts to human understanding. He proposed that mass could be converted to energy and vice versa. His formulation of the equation $E=mc^2$ expresses the mathematical relationship between mass and energy. Some of the concepts that flowed from Einstein's theory of relativity and other works are the idea that space and time are interrelated, gravity "bends" space, and the speed at which something travels bends space and time. His theory of relativity began to open the door to the understanding that everything in the universe is interconnected through some superfield.

Quantum Mechanics

Quantum mechanics is a field of physics that began to really develop in the mid-1900s. With it came some really mind-bending propositions. One of its most interesting findings is the property of entanglement. When two particles become "entangled," effects on one of the particles instantly influence the other particle, no matter how far apart they may be. Quantum mechanics also mathematically uncovered the presence of the zero point field, a field that appeared to contain continuous, subtle electromagnetic energy that exists everywhere, even in a vacuum. According to zero point field theory, there is no place that does not contain energy.

String Theory

String theory replaces the previous particle theory of how atoms and molecules work and replaces them with "strings" that are viewed as expressers of vibration. These vibrations give rise to all subatomic particles and, hence, all matter. Through this view, the universe is a vibrating ocean of energy.

In a drastically oversimplified sense, we are all much like ducks on a pond. When we paddle and splash and move about, we send out ripples across the water. Those ripples can be felt by every other duck on the pond. The implications coming from scientific research are that our thoughts themselves are ripples.

In her comparative review of Connor and Schwartz's work,

McTaggart helps illuminate how our minds and thoughts influence, and are influenced by, the "quantum ocean." In her view, successful healers studied by Schwartz and Connor exhibited significant fluctuations in very low pulsations of a magnetic field coming from their hands. When the results were compared with untrained people attempting healing, the healers produced much greater fluctuations. Two things became clear: people are both transmitters and receivers of electrostatic and magnetic energy, and practice improves a person's ability to manipulate that energy.

Science is now telling us that our thoughts travel out like waves on the quantum ocean. Waves interact with each other both constructively and destructively. When two peaks overlap each other, their effect is cumulative. If their peaks are of equal strength, the resulting overlap will be twice as strong as either of the individual peaks. If a peak overlaps a trough, and their respective strengths are equal, each will cancel the other out. When waves are aligned so that they are in harmony (the peaks line up on top of each other), they are said to be in coherence. The result is a significant increase in their intensity, or power. Pointing to William A. Tiller's example as a good illustration, McTaggart goes on to extend its implications:

> As one scientist put it, coherence is like comparing the photons of a single 60-watt lightbulb to the sun. Ordinarily, light is extraordinarily inefficient. The intensity of light from a bulb is only about 1 watt per square centimeter of light because many of the waves made by the photons destructively interfere with and cancel out each other. The

light generated per square centimeter by the sun is about 6,000 times stronger. But if you could get all the photons of this one small lightbulb to become coherent and resonate in harmony with each other, the energy density of the single lightbulb would be thousands to millions of times higher than that of the surface of the sun.[30]

As our thoughts proceed to a higher order, they become much more powerful. Moreover, as they emit electromagnetic energy, our thoughts appear to travel across space and time. Studies of psycho-kinesis reveal that mental influence produces measurable effects that appear to be unimpeded by distance or even time. By those criteria, highly coherent thoughts may have unlimited influence.

What emerges is a view of thought that points to the exponential growth in influence as thinking proceeds to higher-ordered states. As our thoughts move toward higher order, they increase their ability to entrain other thoughts, increase in energetic power, and extend the distance over which they travel. It is no wonder that elevating consciousness is such a powerful endeavor. This view also underscores the importance and power of our individual contribution to the whole as we elevate our own consciousness. Our thoughts, through coherence, become more powerful, and thus, we as individuals positively contribute to the raising of other people's thoughts through entrainment. Ironically, one of the greatest gifts we can give ourself AND the planet is to elevate our consciousness.

Questions for Group or Individual Exploration

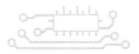

1. What are some of the ways in which Gandhi's accomplishments were remarkable?

2. In what ways does the ego serve as our protector?

3. In doing so, what does it protect?

4. What comparisons can we make between the ego and dictators from history?

5. In what ways might the ego be like a prison cell?

6. What relationships might be inferred between higher-ordered brain patterns and greater objectivity?

7. In what ways might higher-ordered thoughts be considered more powerful?

8. How might a single person, by significantly raising his or her consciousness, affect society?

Meditation as a Tool

While elevating consciousness holds such great promise on so many different levels, we are still faced with the pragmatic question of how to do it. If we approach this question from the perspective of constructing a paradigm, it makes sense to look first at what works. Meditation has proven itself as one of the most effective exercises for raising consciousness. McTaggart says that "meditation makes the brain permanently more coherent."[31]

As meditators gain more control over their thoughts and mental processes, they are able to quiet the mental chatter that is normally present in the background of the mind. They also improve their ability to selectively focus their attention on more and more subtle thoughts and impulses. In doing so, they train their minds to "hear" the still, quiet voice that so many mystic and religious visionaries have pointed to as our connection point with the divine. Many scientists conjecture that the still, quiet voice may well include signals from the quantum field. If, indeed, all of life is the interplay of consciousness and energy, the implied connection is profound. McTaggart explains:

> Mindful meditation enables its practitioners to become aware of unconscious processes, and to remain exquisitely sensitive to external stimuli. As these studies indicate, certain types of concentrated focus, like meditation, enlarge the mechanism by which we receive information and clarify the perception. We turn into a larger, more sensitive radio.[32]

What Is Meditation?

Many people are unfamiliar with exactly what meditation is. Across the world, many schools and methods of meditation have developed. Some meditation methods focus on breath or body awareness. Some focus on stress reduction, healing, or general health and longevity. Other methods focus on quieting the mind and emotions, developing psychic skills, or cultivating spiritual experiences. There is no one right way to meditate. The Sunrise Meditation Method (a method I developed, which is detailed in Appendix A) summarizes a simple, "garden variety" approach to meditation that may prove helpful to those just starting. The purpose of this particular method of meditation is to help people begin the journey toward higher consciousness. It includes both a conceptual framework and specific actions to facilitate the rapid development of one's ability to effectively meditate. It suggests several exercises that assist in establishing habits and skills that will lay the groundwork for self-development of consciousness. While all of the processes of the Sunrise Meditation Method work together to promote the elevation of consciousness, the core essence of the meditation is to develop the ability to quiet the mind and deepen and broaden the person's awareness. Many have claimed that in its purest and simplest form, meditation IS awareness.

In the quietness of meditation, we are able to become aware of deeper layers of ourselves than we can consciously focus on in the hustle and bustle of daily life. As we become aware of these deeper and subtler layers of ourselves, we gain deeper insight into the mental forces that animate us. By better perceiving our inner drives, we gain a greater ability to understand ourselves and thereby satisfy the full range of desires we harbor. Subconscious conflicts in our thinking and beliefs can be brought to the surface and harmoniously resolved once we are aware of their presence. This harmonizing of our mental energy produces much more coherent brain/mind patterns.

Minimizing Negatives; Maximizing Positives

Later in this book, the Twenty-One Indices of Consciousness are covered in detail. The Twenty-One Indices represent twenty-one mental traits that are incredibly effective at raising individual consciousness. They do so by training the mind to use mental patterns that have been shown to be effective and efficient methods of processing energy. Said another way, they are effective mental habits for processing our experiences in a way that minimizes "negatives" and maximizes "positives." Sometimes the positives are things like making us enjoy an experience more. Sometimes the positives come in the form of minimizing the mental and emotional energy we waste on things over which we have no control. Sometimes the positives come in the form of making us a lot more enjoyable for other people to be around, with the social consequences of that being obvious. The Twenty-One Indices represent a "checklist" of traits of higher consciousness, which serves as a good tool for using an organized approach to raising consciousness. When meditation is used as a means to contemplate the working of the Twenty-One Indices within the practitioner's mind, the two processes work together synergistically. Their combined contributions can significantly speed the evolution of consciousness.

Questions for Group or Individual Exploration

1. What does "meditation" mean for you?

2. What are some of the benefits of meditation that you have heard other people describe?

3. Describe what experiences you have had with meditation.

4. What is the connection between meditation and greater mental coherence?

5. How would you predict that meditation might aid a person in achieving greater mental coherence?

6. What other practices are you aware of that you would say are similar to meditation? What are the purposes of those practices?

Scaling the Mountain
of Needs

Maslow's Hierarchy of Needs

As our meditation takes us into deeper levels of ourselves and makes us more aware of our environment, what do we do with all this new information? We of course use it to improve our quality of life experience, making ourselves happier. Some helpful suggestions on how to go about this come from the field of psychology. The psychologist Abraham Maslow devised a conceptual structure for viewing human drives and motivations. His structure became famously known as Maslow's Hierarchy of Needs. Within this hierarchy, Maslow laid out what he believed were some of the major motivating forces within the human psyche. The needs were broken into categories, with the categories stacked on top of each other. Maslow's view was that people progress through the levels (from bottom to top) much as a student progresses from first grade to fifth grade. One grade had to be successfully completed before moving on to the next grade. According to Maslow's hierarchy, the needs in a category are more primary and urgent than those in the categories above it. Consequently, the needs of a level must be satisfied before needs on the next level can be addressed. Figure 1 is a generalized picture of Maslow's hierarchy:

Fig. 1. Maslow's famous hierarchy.

We see, for example, that the first level on Maslow's hierarchy of needs is physiological needs. Based on Maslow's research, we will generally need to feel that our physiological needs are satisfied before we can or will pursue satisfying our safety needs. Once we have satisfied physiological needs, we will then automatically begin efforts to satisfy our safety needs. Thus, we move up the mountain, climbing one category at a time. The first two tiers of needs, physiological and safety, are, for most people, merely maintenance requirements. It's not until we get to the top three tiers that we begin to hit "pay dirt." In general, the higher the tier of need, the more sublime is the person's satisfaction in satisfying that need. The goal, according to Maslow, is to move up the hierarchy so that we can address the furthest-reaching human need: self-actualization. A self-actualized person is one who expresses the fullness of his or her potential and is living life at his or her highest capacity.

The Path of Conquest

The obvious question is, "How do we climb this mountain and achieve the peak state of self-actualization?" At the granular level, we undertake the actions in life that will meet our physiological needs. For most people, this entails either finding and working at a job that will pay enough money to pay for groceries, utilities, and living space or being in a relationship with another person who will assist in paying those expenses for them. Having done that, the person then looks to satisfy his or her safety needs. This often comes in the form of selecting a neighborhood and housing that the person deems adequately secure to feel safe. Insurance is often used as a key component in the safety arsenal. The person may also purchase a burglar, fire, and/or car alarm. Others will avail themselves of other personal safety measures.

Once our safety needs have been satisfied, we then go to work attempting to satisfy our love and belonging needs. We make efforts to find and sustain relationships that will make us feel valued within those relationships. Suitable companions for a satisfying intimate relationship are sought; in many cultures, this often takes place through dating and courtship. Once we have formed relationships that meet our love and belonging needs, we then start to pursue satisfying our esteem needs. We work to secure the respect and admiration of others. While the urge and need is similar among people, the means by which people seek to satisfy their esteem needs begin to become more of an individualistic thing. Different people will seek respect in significantly different ways and from different sets of peers.

Once we have satisfied our esteem needs, we then will work at satisfying our self-actualization needs. Here, at the peak of the mountain, the needs become extremely individualistic. Arguably, the exact composition of each person's manner of satisfying his or her self-actualization needs is unique to that individual alone.

This process of undertaking actions to acquire the things, relationships, and reputations that will satisfy our needs can be referred to as the Path of Conquest, as shown in figure 2:

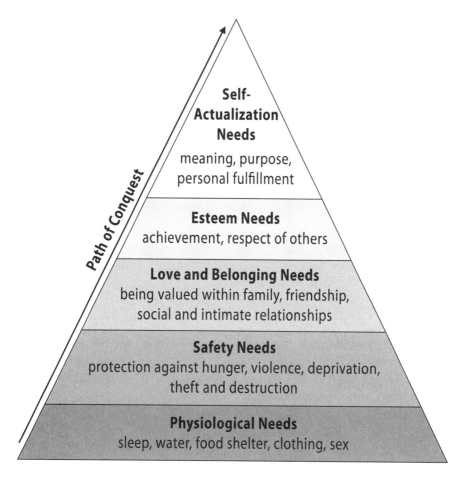

Fig. 2. The Path of Conquest.

We work to obtain opportunities and resources, which we can then convert into something that satisfies our needs. By diligently applying our efforts to our environment, we gradually increase our power and control over it. As our control increases, we are able to avail ourselves of the resources and relationships required to satisfy our needs. In this way, we methodically climb the mountain toward the peak of self-actualization. However, this is the path of the ego. In very simplistic terms, this is the path of our animal nature growing out of the law of the jungle: exert oneself in order to gain control over the external environment and other people so we can get what we want to satisfy our needs. It is the path of assertion, conquest, and domination. But as with most things, there is more than one way to skin a cat.

The Path of Transformation

Another path is the Path of Transformation. While it moves us up the same mountain, it does so via another route, as shown in figure 3.

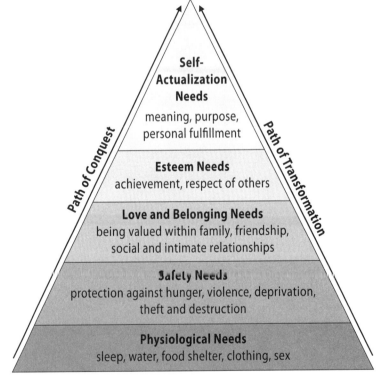

Fig. 3. The Path of Transformation provides another "route" up the "mountain."

Instead of focusing on gaining power over the external environment, the Path of Transformation focuses on changing the inner landscape. Instead of climbing to the peak of a giant mountain of needs, we flatten the mountain and bring the peak down to us. By changing what we view as our needs, we can satisfy them by lessening their demands. This is the path we often see reflected in many spiritual and religious traditions. In simplistic terms, it can be viewed as the path of our spiritual nature. It derives its power not from controlling our external environment and others, but from controlling ourselves.

As an extreme example, consider those who have been clinically diagnosed as paranoid. They believe that virtually everyone is out to do them harm in some way. Because they see the world as completely full of threats, they have an extremely elevated safety need. Their need is so high, in fact, that they could spend all of their time trying to make themselves feel safe and not succeed. What is the result of this highly elevated need for safety? According to Maslow's hierarchy, they will never be able to effectively pursue satisfying their love and belonging needs. In other words, they will never experience quality relationships. All of their attention and energy will be consumed in a futile quest to feel safe.

However, let's now assume that a sufferer has been completely cured of his or her paranoia. With even a modest job, the person is now likely to be able to satisfy his or her safety needs. Thus satisfied, the person is free to pursue satisfying love and belonging needs through meaningful relationships. While this example is extreme, it does illustrate the point. This person flattened an insurmountable barrier, merely by changing how he or she viewed the world. The person changed nothing about the environment, only himself or herself. This is the Path of Transformation.

In much more subtle ways, we have all kinds of opportunities to flatten the mountain of needs and arrive at self-actualization. Consider another example, Carl and Will. Carl and Will both want to be respected. However, in their thinking, they use different methods of determining whether they are respected. For Carl, being respected is being seen as a successful businessman by his peers. This sets Carl up in a catch-22 of keeping up with the Joneses. Carl's peers, in typical fashion, determine success by external signifiers, like membership in the country club, the car Carl drives, and the size of his house. So to be seen as successful and thus respected, and to get his esteem needs met, Carl (to show his success) joins the country club and buys a nicer car. This requires Carl to earn more money to pay the increase in expenses. Being so successful, Carl's circle of friends grows as he's introduced to "bigger wigs."

His new business associates and friends move in bigger circles, and of course have bigger, nicer homes. True to his own values, Carl holds more respect for the more successful friends, so those are the relationships he pursues. Carl buys a bigger house in which to entertain and impress his new friends so his new peers will view him as successful at their level and his esteem needs will be met. Carl has to make yet again more money to pay the increased mortgage. Over time, the circle turns again, and Carl now has to buy a mansion and a yacht. The end result is Carl's mountain of need growing taller and taller at the esteem level.

Will, on the other hand, measures respect by being seen as a good father to his children. Will is loving and nurturing to them.

He attends all their games and is involved in PTA. Will teaches his children values, manners, and the importance of hard work and respect for others. Will is occasionally approached by parents who say how wonderful his children are and what an excellent father he must be. Other parents in the neighborhood want their children playing at Will's house with his kids because it's "such a good environment." Will's Esteem needs are satisfied and Will is freed up to work on self-actualization.

At least with regard to the esteem level, Carl's mountain of needs is MUCH larger than Will's. Will is going to have a much easier time approaching self-actualization than Carl is. This is not because Will has been more successful in overcoming his environment. In fact, from the facts given, Carl has been able to exert much more control over his environment than Will has. Nevertheless, Will is getting more of his needs met. The crucially important difference is in how these men chose to define their esteem needs.

Our conscious and subconscious minds are filled with dozens if not hundreds of such needs criteria. We, at some level, define what for ourselves these needs are. And what we believe has a huge impact on the size of our mountain. The tricky part is that most of these factors are embedded in our subconscious and affect our thinking without our being consciously aware of the impact they are having. Elevating consciousness is about becoming consciously aware of what our inner values and criteria actually are and consciously shaping them into what we intend for them to be. Otherwise we are operating on a haphazardly assembled value set which may not serve us well.

The Path of Conquest and the Path of Transformation are both valid approaches to getting our needs met and thereby being happy. But whether we pursue the Path of Conquest, the Path of Transformation, or a judicious balance and blending of the two, we should pursue it with full awareness and intention. If we allow ourselves to drift, it is quite easy for the Path of Conquest to become destructive, the mountain of desire to grow to unscalable heights, or the Path of Transformation to limit our interaction with the world.

Questions for Group or Individual Exploration

1. How have you observed Maslow's hierarchy of needs applying in your own life?

2. How have you observed Maslow's hierarchy of needs applying in other people's lives?

3. At this point in your life, what would self-actualization look like for you?

4. What are some ways you have seen people use the Path of Conquest to satisfy their needs?

5. What are some ways you have seen people use the Path of Transformation to satisfy their needs?

6. What are some of the benefits and weaknesses of each of the two paths?

7. What are some of your need assumptions that might be hindering your ability to satisfy and thus climb your mountain of needs?

Charting the Map of Consciousness

While the Path of Conquest and the Path of Transformation are both important and valuable approaches, this book focuses primarily on the Path of Transformation, not because the Path of Conquest is less important, but because of the limited scope of this book. In examining the Path of Transformation, it is clear that its focus is on how we think and what we believe—and on how those things affect what we feel our needs are. By taking control of ourselves, we can control the height of the mountain we must climb to be satisfied and happy. But it is not simply about doing without, the first conclusion we would normally come to. Rather, it is about qualitative changes more than quantitative changes. It is one thing to try and reduce the mountain by saying, "I don't need to be loved." That is effectively a denial of a basic human need. It is another thing entirely to say, "I am changing what I believe about what love is, and even if people don't treat me exactly the way I want them to, I accept that they are loving me to the best of their ability." Or we could change our view from, "Love is a resource that other people give me," to, "Love is something I create and a state of mind I maintain."

There are countless such "view options" available for a long list of common human concerns. Useful paradigms help us organize and streamline these views into a form where they become apparent, useable, and more efficient. One of the major difficulties people encounter is a conflict in their subconscious choices and assumptions. Underneath the surface, their beliefs and desires waste enormous amounts of energy competing with each other, and often this waste manifests as self-sabotaging or self-limiting behavior. Eliminating these subconscious conflicts is a major source of increased personal power. Paradigms help us explore, clarify, and shape the way our minds think. The best resources for constructing paradigms are succinct summaries of accumulated human wisdom. These pearls of wisdom can compress volumes of insight into a simple, easy-to-use form, or tenet. The perennial advice of the golden rule—"Do unto others as you would have others do unto you"—is a prime example. The reasons why this is a beneficial tenet to hold are virtually countless. Love serves the individual. Love serves society. Additionally, as modern science is coming to understand, love also directs energy itself. For the greatest efficiency, the tenets of a paradigm should fit seamlessly together, forming a consistent and harmonious model with which to engage life. Simplicity is another key ingredient, as simplicity is a great boon to ease of use and effective application. With the paradigm of elevating consciousness, we work free of the hopeless constrictors of expressing absolute truth, and instead we are free to focus on what is effective.

A Historical Perspective

Fortunately, history has compiled for us an extensive record of approaches and ideas that have shown themselves effective in improving the human experience of life. History has applied its litmus test of time to highlight for our benefit many individuals who have shown themselves to have achieved a high degree of order in their thoughts—people like Krishna, Socrates, Buddha, Jesus, Epictetus, Gandhi, Rumi, Newton, King, Lao Tzu, and Einstein, to name a few. These and other remarkable individuals, because of the power of their thoughts, have left a legacy of wisdom and understanding that has carried humanity forward and kept these individuals alive in our collective awareness. From this extensive storehouse of insights, the tenets of this paradigm have been drawn. Certainly it doesn't represent all of them, but it does represent some of the most common hallmarks in the realm of higher-ordered thinking. When a view or concept emerges as an anchor of wisdom surfacing across many epochs and cultures, it stands out as a prime candidate for inclusion. From these gems, the paradigm of elevating consciousness has been assembled. As an illustrative example, the golden rule serves well. This principle has surfaced many times in numerous cultures as a wise principle to live by. One of the most familiar forms is that taught by Jesus: "Do unto others as you would have others do unto you." An example from an early Egyptian papyrus reads, "That which you hate to be done to you, do not do to another." In ancient Greece, Sextus taught, "What you wish your neighbors to be to you, such be also to them." Baha'u'llah taught, "Ascribe not to any soul, that which thou would not have ascribed to thee." Confucius taught, "Never impose on others what you would not choose for yourself." The Hindu scriptures teach, "One should never do that to another which one regards as injurious to one's own self" (Anusanana Parva, Section CXIII, Verse 8). Muhammad said, "Hurt no one so that no one may hurt you." From the Torah comes, "Love your neighbor as yourself." From Buddhism comes the teaching, "Hurt not others in ways that you yourself would find hurtful" (Udana-Varga 5:18). Native American Black Elk taught, "All things are our relatives; what we do to everything, we do to ourselves. All is really One." From Zoroastrianism comes, "Whatever is disagreeable to yourself, do not do unto others" (Shayast-na-Shayast 13:29). The golden rule is a principle of conduct in relation to others. It is a simple maxim, yet, if followed, it can have a profound impact on society and individual relationships. There is good reason why this principle has been independently and recurrently advocated in cultures across the globe. However, as powerful a principle as it is, it is directed at conduct and therefore falls into the domain of ethics.

Tenets of the Consciousness Paradigm are aimed at thought rather than conduct, as thought is the seed from which conduct sprouts. Moreover, our thoughts, whether we act on them or not, have the power to cause us pleasure or pain. Hence, Black Elk's rendition of the golden rule provides a viewpoint best suited for a tenet of the Consciousness Paradigm: "All things are connected as One." While this is less, or even nonspecific, in terms of appropriate conduct, it provides much greater guidance through a viewpoint that, if adopted, will in itself guide conduct as well as thought. As is discussed in other sections of this book, the idea that all things are connected as one is a central concept of the Consciousness Paradigm. Like the Golden Rule, this concept has appeared in many cultures. In Native American tradition, it is exemplified by Black Elk's teaching. The ancient Aitareya Upanishads taught it:

> This Self is all in all. He is all the gods, the five elements, earth, air, fire, water, and space; all creatures, great or small, born of eggs, of wombs, of heat, of shoots; horses, cows, elephants, men and women; all beings that walk, all beings that fly, and all that neither walk nor fly. Prajna is pure consciousness, guiding all.

Jesus taught it when he said, "Father, keep through thine own name those whom thou hast given me, that they may be one, as we are" (John 17:11), and, "On that day you will realize that I am in my Father, and you are in me, and I am in you" (John 14:20).

We also see the principle proposed by modern physics, not as a philosophical precept, but as a paradigm for viewing the substrata of physical reality:

O

A human being is part of the whole, called by us "universe,"
a part limited in time and space. He experiences himself, his thoughts
and feelings as something separated from the rest—a kind of optical
delusion of his consciousness.

—Albert Einstein

O

On the same subject McTaggart says, "The universe was not a storehouse of static, separate objects, but a single organism of interconnected energy fields in a continuous state of becoming."[33] This viewpoint, or way of looking at the world, is a simple maxim, yet it offers great guidance and assistance as a perspective from which to process reality. It becomes harder to hate another when we view them as extensions of ourselves. And inoculating ourselves against hate is one of the healthiest things we can do for ourselves and our peace of mind.

Another example that is discussed extensively in this book is the principle of open-mindedness. While the principle is simple, the benefits that can be reaped by maintaining an open state of mind are immense. Many great thinkers, from Socrates to Feynman, have reveled in its benefits.

The Desire for Happiness

One of the most basic and widely recognized motivators in life is the desire for happiness. Ask almost any of us, "If you had to choose, and you could only have one for yourself, would you choose _____ [fill in the blank], OR would you rather be happy?" We will, after thinking about it, almost always choose happiness. In the end, happiness is what we are all after. Happiness is the gold at the end of the rainbow—on that we can almost all agree. What we don't agree on is the path that will take us there. Each person's path is unique. There are, however, certain factors that strongly affect a person's ability to experience happiness. These factors have proven themselves over thousands of years of human investigation, contemplation, and trial and error. While many things, experiences, and relationships can contribute to happiness, these are just the surface of a deeper reality. History and even everyday experience are filled with different people living extremely similar lives, yet some of these people are very happy, some are very unhappy, and many are neither. Clearly, the commonalities that happy people possess lie below the surface of what we commonly observe. The goal is to peel back the veneer that covers the surface and causes, for most people, so much confusion and expose the deeper realities that happy people are using to their advantage.

The ability to consistently experience happiness is not a matter of luck or good fortune. It is not determined by one's circumstances in life. It is determined by a person's ability to perceive and use those deeper levels of reality that form the mold for how we experience life. By far, the single most effective thing one can use to achieve a happy, fulfilling life is called "consciousness." Consciousness is the breadth, depth, and clarity of one's perception of "reality" and the effective use of those perceptions together with available resources, thoughts, and skills.

The single biggest predictor of the amount of happiness and satisfaction one will experience in life is the Level of Consciousness at which one functions. Consciousness, more so than any other factor, determines people's ability to travel the unique path that will bring them happiness. This has proven true across individuals, cultures, and time.

Elevating Consciousness to Reduce the Negative and Increase the Positive

Elevating consciousness reduces negative emotions such as pain, fear, anxiety, anger, and stress. In many cases, these can be eliminated almost entirely. At the same time, elevating consciousness increases the positive emotions of peace, love, and joy. Higher consciousness also significantly increases such positive traits as creativity, wisdom, clarity of life purpose, insight, and intuition. It brings better relationships and a more profound experience of love. While these claims may seem too good to be true, they are not. These treasures are available to anyone who wants them, but there is a price that must be paid.

The difficulty with raising consciousness is that it is not a quick fix. It takes hard work and development over time, as does mastery of any major discipline. It requires people to maintain brutal self-honesty, face their fears, and repeatedly step outside their comfort zone. This hurdle has been steep enough to keep the vast majority of people at bay. At the same time, most people have never been taught what the payoffs are and how they get them.

It can take months or years to advance a single level in consciousness. And although the evolution of people's consciousness is neither easy nor quick, the benefits pay out over the rest of their life. People who operate at evolved levels of consciousness not only experience a better life, they also make more positive contributions to the people with whom they have relationships. Put another way, they make better friends, mates, parents, and members of society. Consequently, they have greater access to relationships with others who are functioning at more developed levels of consciousness. As the saying goes, birds of a feather flock together.

One of the greatest influences on our lives is the relationships we have. As our Level of Consciousness evolves, our beliefs, habits, and practices that are destructive and offensive to other people diminish and subside. At the same time, our ability to positively contribute to other people's lives increases. When we operate at higher levels of consciousness, we are also much better equipped to identify others who are operating at higher levels of consciousness. Because of this, our ability to choose quality relationships is significantly improved. If we spent half as much time assessing a potential mate's Level of Consciousness as we do his or her physical and personality traits, the odds of finding Mr. or Mrs. Right would increase dramatically, as would our odds of avoiding Mr. or Mrs. Wrong. Understanding, using, and being able to assess consciousness is one of the single most useful tools we can have in our pursuit of happiness.

From an organizational standpoint, employees or group members who function at higher levels of consciousness are significantly less likely to engage in counterproductive or destructive behaviors that damage the group as a whole. On the upside, their ability to understand and relate to other people is typically quite good, strengthening the cohesiveness and effectiveness of their group.

Fortunately, there are certain landmarks that highlight the route to higher consciousness. These landmarks have surfaced from thousands of years of efforts to map the human mind and emotions. Pioneers in philosophy, religion, mysticism, psychology, and metaphysics have recorded observations and insights from their work and research. Despite undertaking their journeys from many diverse starting points, they have consistently encountered and described certain common landmarks. When viewed from a bigger picture, these milestones show the way.

In an effort to arrive at an understandable and useful map of consciousness, an organized framework will be used. At its most basic, this framework is made up of Levels of Consciousness. These levels, stacked one on top of the other, can be thought of as a ladder. All of us emerge as infants functioning on the bottom rung of the consciousness ladder. As we mature and grow, our consciousness evolves, and we climb the ladder rung by rung, progressing through higher Levels of Consciousness. At each level, we are able to use that Level of Consciousness and every Level of Consciousness below it. However, until we have developed our ability in a given Level of Consciousness, its powers and benefits remain largely inaccessible. While, in reality, the dividing lines between the levels are arbitrary divisions in a continuum, they do serve as a useful if somewhat simplified map. Ken Wilbur, in his work *Integral Psychology*, has masterfully compared numerous views and schools of thought on consciousness that span thousands of years and many cultures. Once past the language, the similarity in views is striking. While some adjustments and substitutions have been made here, by and large Wilbur's work serves as the blueprint for the map.

Breaking the continuum of consciousness into levels is helpful in providing a comparative reference for where on the hierarchy our consciousness is functioning. This aids in determining the route we have traveled and the milestones to aim for on the journey forward. As any experience with a map will show, knowing where one is going and having a route to get there drastically increases the odds of actually arriving. The only question remaining is whether we will have the heart and desire to make the journey. These levels of consciousness can be thought of as the "global" view of our map of consciousness.

In *Integral Psychology*, Wilbur summarizes the combined works and studies of Clare Graves, Don Beck, and Christopher Cowen, as they relate to levels of conscious development. Although some level names have been changed in this work to make them more familiar, the structure is derived directly from their work. The developmental levels have, through extensive research, been found to be present and consistent within many sample groups across the globe. From the research, estimates have been made as to the percentage of the world's population that is functioning at each level. The levels of consciousness, numbered in descending order from highest to lowest, are as follows:

Level of Consciousness	Percentage of World's Population Functioning Primarily at This Level
The Harmonic Range of Consciousness	
7. Transcendent	0.1%
6. Integral	1.0%
The Competitive Range of Consciousness	
5. Pluralistic	10%
4. Rational	30%
3. Conformist	40%
2. Individualist	20%
1. Instinctual	10%

Table 1. Percentage operating at each level.

The percentage total exceeds 100 percent, as some people are on the cusp and span two levels. Graves, Beck, and Cowan point out that the levels of consciousness from the most basic (instinctual) up through pluralistic are self-defensive. These levels constitute the Competitive Range of Consciousness. People functioning within the Competitive Range generally see their Level of Consciousness, or their approach to life, as the right way, superior to the others. This sets up an inherent conflict among people who are functioning at different levels within the Competitive Range. This is one of the most fundamental issues underlying conflict in relationships because, as we will see later, it means their worldviews, and thus essentially their worlds, are quite different. At a subconscious level, it takes them off the same page.

This subtle conflict lies below the surface and is therefore seldom recognized. But because it forms the foundation of how we view and react to life, it influences almost everything in our life. It influences the decisions we make and how we view and behave within relationships. If a person operating within the Competitive Range of Consciousness wants to find a smooth and near-effortless relationship, he or she should be careful about selecting someone functioning at a different Level of Consciousness within the Competitive Range. While choosing a relationship with someone on the same level as oneself will not guarantee common views and a consistently smooth interaction, establishing a relationship with someone functioning in another level virtually guarantees some inherent conflict that otherwise would not exist. People at different levels within the Competitive Range will, at a subconscious level, view things and make decisions in a fundamentally different way. While the wisdom that can come from the interplay of diverse views can be a strength, it still requires good skills in communication and conflict resolution from both people involved. It also increases the relational "overhead" and should be taken into account in relationship evaluations.

The second range of consciousness, The Harmonic Range, includes the integral and transcendent Levels of Consciousness. People functioning within this range generally appreciate the values of each Level of Consciousness and recognize the importance of each within the whole. Having recognized value in each level, they are able to more effectively assess each level's strengths and weaknesses in given circumstances and relationships. Instead of being stuck within the belief that they are using the best tool (Level of Consciousness) in the toolbox and seeking improvement solely by increasing their skill with that tool, the whole toolbox becomes available to them. (As discussed earlier, one has access not only to the Level of Consciousness in which one is primarily functioning, but to each Level of Consciousness below that.) Consequently, those functioning within the harmonic range are better equipped to use the best tool for the task at hand and can build much more complex, elegant, and effective approaches for interacting with their reality. They are also much more effective at relating to and interacting with people who are not functioning at their level.

The story has been told that Henry Ford, in explaining his success with the assembly line manufacture of cars, said, "I really don't know anything about building a car." He admitted he didn't know how to best assemble a drive train. Nor did he know how best to build an engine. Nor did he know much about the machinery that automated the assembly process. "But what I do know," he said, "is that if I push this button on my desk, I can get the best engineers in the country to tell me about engines. And if I push this button, I can get the best mechanics to tell me the best ways of putting cars together. And if I push this button, I can get the best salespeople to tell me how to sell these things." Metaphorically speaking, Ford could be thought of as the integral Level of Consciousness, being informed by and coordinating the expertise of lower, more focused levels of consciousness. By overseeing and coordinating all of the different "intelligences," he was able to create a system that revolutionized the globe. In a similar manner, higher consciousness appreciates and uses the strengths of each of the lower levels of consciousness rather than asserts itself as superior to them. It is the effective, harmonious integration that provides the true power.

Questions for Group or Individual Exploration

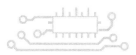

1. What are some ways in which eliminating internal conflicts can increase personal power?

2. What are some "life-view options" you have seen others claim that were in conflict with each other? How did this affect them?

3. What are some "life-view options" you have chosen that may be in conflict with each other? How might this affect you?

4. Based on your observations, how would you say most people view others who have significant inconsistencies in their approach to, or beliefs about, life?

5. Using the analogy of tools for the Seven Levels of Consciousness, in what ways might higher levels of consciousness make people happier?

The Seven Levels of Consciousness

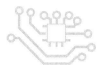

As previously mentioned, each Level of Consciousness has its own strengths and weaknesses. Each level represents a global conceptual framework through which the world and events in life can be viewed and interpreted. A very simplified characterization of each of the levels of consciousness follows, from lowest to highest. It comes as no surprise that, in general terms they are reminiscent of and harmonious with Maslow's hierarchy.

The Competitive Range of Consciousness

The Instinctual Level.

This is the most basic and fundamental level of human consciousness and is not much more than the survival instinct. This level is reactionary and focuses on the acquisition of the basic resources necessary to sustain life. Conflicts for people functioning at this Level of Consciousness are typically viewed as, and sometimes are, struggles with life and death ramifications.

The Individualist Level.

This Level of Consciousness centers on the defense and advancement of the ego as the apex of physical consciousness. People functioning at this level are focused on the avoidance or elimination of threats. This frequently surfaces as a need to control their environment and other people. Failure to have control is viewed as a grave detriment to the person's ego and security. At this Level of Consciousness, the person's ego and security are typically undifferentiated from his or her perceived well-being.

The Conformist Level.

This Level of Consciousness centers on the need for acceptance and often manifests as a tribal mentality. Members of the perceived tribe are valued over others, as "tribal members" offer the support system individuals perceive themselves as needing. While relationships become important in and of themselves, persons outside the tribe are viewed as less important, inferior, or even dangerous. The Conformist Level of Consciousness often carries a strong emphasis on compliance with tribal rules and customs. The importance of these codes of conduct are evaluated by their level of acceptance within the tribe rather than by the merit of the rules themselves. The tribe or clan can be any type of identifiable group. It could be a family network, a religious group, or even a socioeconomic class. It can be any group with which the individual strongly identifies.

The Rational Level.

At this Level of Consciousness, formal rational thinking predominates. Logic and reason are employed in evaluating situations and relationships. Rules are measured in terms of fairness, justice, and effectiveness. The scope of consideration for applying these values typically extends beyond tribal boundaries.

The Pluralistic Level.

At this Level of Consciousness, an egalitarian view predominates and people are valued because they are human beings, not because they are right or excel at some particular trait. Empathy becomes a globally useable skill and can be extended to any human being.

The Harmonic Range of Consciousness

The Integral Level.

At this Level of Consciousness, the inherent value of all people and all levels of consciousness becomes apparent. The dispassionate reason of the Rational Level and the nonrational love of the Pluralistic Level are viewed as integral components of an effectively functioning whole. The various views, approaches, and considerations of all the levels of consciousness are seen to function harmoniously rather than competitively.

The Transcendent Level.

At this Level of Consciousness, a sense of the divinity of all things emerges. Perception shifts from the harmonic interaction of disparate parts as seen from the Integral Level to a holistic view of all reality. All parts of the universe are seen as one organic whole expressing itself in limitless ways.

Consciousness as a Ladder

Just like our bodies grow, as our consciousness grows, it gets "bigger." Having viewed the seven levels of consciousness, we get the picture of a "ladder" of consciousness with seven rungs. This ladder is ascended as a person's consciousness grows. Similar to the climb up a real ladder, the higher we go on the consciousness ladder, the further we can "see." The Consciousness Calculator is a program that makes a general assessment of the Level of Consciousness at which a person is functioning. A free, downloadable copy is available on my Web site at www.AppliedConsciousnessSystems.com.

Consciousness as a Spectrum

In reality, consciousness is a spectrum. This spectrum begins with a single point of awareness and concern. As it grows and develops, it extends outward. A young child is a good example of a person functioning as a single point of consciousness. She is aware of and concerned for her desires and only her desires. The child is unable to consider her impact on others, much less other people's perceptions.

But as the child's consciousness develops, she becomes aware of her effect on her environment and on other people. As a toddler, the child becomes able to understand and learn that biting mother will bring a negative response from her. After further growth and development, the child learns that if she says mean things to her playmates, it may hurt their feelings. With even further development, the child is able to view the situation from the viewpoint of her playmate and think, *If that were said to me, it would hurt my feelings*. Now the child is able to view the world from two perspectives: her own and as the prospective recipient of her actions. Simplistically speaking, the child's consciousness has now doubled. She can understand and consider two perspectives, whereas before she could only handle one.

With further development and growth of consciousness, the child can consider how a third person might view her interaction with a playmate. She can understand how saying mean things to a playmate might cause anger in the third person toward her and sympathy for her target. So the child's consciousness can now handle three perspectives. And so it goes as consciousness grows. The higher the Level of Consciousness, the broader and more diverse the points of view the child can value and effectively consider. She will also become more accurate in deciphering another person's actual perspective. Her savvy and perception skills will grow keener.

As has been said, the simpleton's concern is for his family. The citizen's concern is for his community. The patriot's concern is for his country, and the saint's concern is for humanity. Eventually, as consciousness approaches the top of the ladder, the entire world matters within the person's considerations.

Consciousness in Relationships

Coming back to the scope of individuals, let's take a look at the workings of consciousness within the context of relationships. It is amazing the number of people who marry a "wolf" and then get upset when the wolf behaves like a wolf. If they want a lamb, they should select a lamb. The odds of that approach working well are astronomically higher than one's picking a hyena and expecting it to behave like a rabbit. Many people are seeking "angels" to have relationships with. For purposes of this illustration, angels are people who have, and consistently maintain, the qualities that make them excellent partners in a relationship. In short, if people want angels in their lives, they'd better learn what angels are like so they can choose one. It can take a while to develop the understanding needed to discern an angel, but anyone who has ever thought he or she had found an angel but wound up chained to a hyena can tell you it is more than worth the effort. Metaphorically speaking, people who live at the higher end of the consciousness spectrum are angels. In fact, at very high levels, they are often viewed as saintly. For a long list of reasons, some of which are covered here, if you want a taste of Heaven, spend time with an angel. And when two angels form a tight relationship, the relationship is often perceived by others as "heavenly." It is a pervasive state of relationship bliss and fulfillment that few people ever have the chance to know.

On the downside of the spectrum are "demons," people who are selfish and self-centered. Their consciousness is so underdeveloped that they lack the ability to effectively consider and value viewpoints outside their own. They are frequently either oblivious or indifferent to the pain they cause others; they only care about what benefits them. Being in a serious relationship with someone functioning at a low Level of Consciousness can be like having a relationship with an ill-mannered thirteen-year-old who has all the cunning of a wily politician and the ruthlessness of a robber baron.

Many people complain that at the beginning of a relationship they were "fooled" or "deceived" by the other person into believing that person was something he or she wasn't. This happens frequently when a person is making relationship evaluations based on what's on the surface rather than peeling back the veneer and looking at the real essence of who and what the other person is. This real essence can be summed up by the Level of Consciousness at which the person is functioning.

It goes without saying that in actuality there are no real "demons." People functioning at low levels of consciousness are pursuing the exact same thing as people functioning at higher levels of consciousness. They are both pursuing what they believe will make them happy. The difference is in what combination of actions and beliefs they think will take them there. Knowing what Level of Consciousness a person is functioning at will give you a very good idea of what kinds of actions and beliefs that person is likely to think will bring him or her happiness. Knowing that makes it much easier to anticipate how he or she will view and behave in circumstances he or she encounters. Consequently, if good relationships are an important consideration for people, they would be well advised to develop a good understanding of consciousness and its traits.

Research has shown that relationships are one of the greatest contributors to a person's happiness and experience of a high quality of life. Developing a good understanding of consciousness and being able to tell at what Level of Consciousness another person is functioning enables greater skill in assessing the type of relationship one can expect to have.

As a general rule, relationships between people who are functioning at different levels of consciousness will carry a greater level of inherent strain. This is especially true for the person who is functioning at the higher Level of Consciousness. Being in these types of "different-level" relationships greatly increases the stress a person experiences in life. While there is usually not constant strain within such relationships, it typically intensifies when challenges arise. This is because it is the more important questions and challenges of life that are likely to bring out the differences in views and reactions. For example, when a loved one dies, people at different levels of consciousness are likely to see different meanings in death and, therefore, react to it differently. And so it is with questions of morality and other significant challenges in life. Thus, the relationship is saddled with a built-in stress multiplier that makes its biggest impact exactly at the worst times for it to do so.

Clearly, selectively choosing our close relationships is one of the most important and powerful decisions we make in raising our quality of life. For the vast majority of us, the Level of Consciousness at which we function is the single biggest factor in determining our happiness. It changes how we see the world and the meaning of circumstances and events within it. Since perception is reality as far as the mind is concerned, a change in consciousness literally changes the world we live in. Additionally, our Level of Consciousness forms the core of our skill in choosing relationships. If we are interested in raising our own Level of Consciousness, the consciousness map gives an idea of where we are now. It will also help us identify people who are functioning at higher

Levels of Consciousness. These people can serve as positive points of contact and support for our growth.

Most people, instead of consciously considering their choices, enter relationships based on a "best-case evaluation." The relationship is evaluated in terms of the best experiences culled from the best of circumstances. Dating is a common example. The typical couple evaluates and forms a relationship based on the peak experiences encountered in the dating process, when both parties are frequently striving to impress. A more thorough approach would be to use an "all-case" approach to evaluating the relationship. The reactions and behaviors of the other person should be looked at under all circumstances one is likely to encounter in life. This will give a much more realistic picture of who that person is and how one can expect to be treated by that person in less-than-ideal circumstances. How does the person handle tragedy, grief, and loss; injustices that come his or her way; stress and disaster? And how does this person treat the people that he or she doesn't care about? Although it would be advisable to observe a person in all of these circumstances before making a lifelong commitment to him or her, practically speaking, it may not be possible within the typical period of time encompassed by most courtships. Fortunately, understanding the Level of Consciousness at which a person is functioning can give well-educated predictions and even some answers to the above questions. If one understands the foundation upon which another's attitudes and behaviors are drawn, he or she has a good indicator of what those attitudes and behaviors are likely to be in general terms.

The reason an all-case evaluation is so important is that the people involved in every close relationship, especially dating, mating, and marriage relationships, are likely to experience significant stressors during the course of the relationship. That is a reality of life. In simplistic terms, as long as the two people involved agree on the meaning of and approach to a challenge they encounter, they will view each other as allied. They can be said to be "aligned." However, if they happen to hold different views of the issue, or of how to handle the issue, they will then be "unaligned." This line between being aligned and unaligned is a critically important line to understand. The reason for this is that at lower Levels of Consciousness, the way people treat those with whom they are unaligned is drastically different from how they treat those with whom they are aligned. Odds are extremely high that, for some periods during the course of any relationship, the couple will be unaligned over certain situations. The greater the difference in their Levels of Consciousness, the more frequently this is likely to occur. For any important existing or potential relationship, it is vitally important to understand how that individual is likely to treat you when you find yourselves unaligned.

As an example, let's say Connie is functioning at the Conformist Level of Consciousness, and Tom is a member of her "tribe." Her behavior toward him is likely to generally be amiable, cordial, and supportive. However, if Tom is ousted from the tribe, Connie's behavior toward Tom is thereafter likely to be hostile and suspicious. While Tom may not have changed as a person at all, Connie's attitudes toward and treatment of him are now significantly different—and significantly more negative. This same phenomenon occurs on varying scales within relationships when a person moves from being in alignment to out of alignment. At lower Levels of

Consciousness, there is an underlying assumption: "If you're not with me [if you don't see things the way I see them, and approach things the way I approach them], then you are against me." This is especially true in close relationships in which reliance on the other person is an important part of the relationship. In such cases, if one refuses to march to the other's drum, one is perceived as a deserter, or even worse, a traitor. In evaluating relationships, it would be prudent to have some idea of the likelihood of waking up on any given day as the deserter or traitor.

Questions for Group or Individual Exploration

1. What similarities do you see between Maslow's Hierarchy of Needs and the Seven Levels of Consciousness?

2. What differences do you see between Maslow's Hierarchy of Needs and the Seven Levels of Consciousness?

3. What changes would you expect people to undergo as they progress from the first Level of Consciousness (the instinctual level) up to the Seventh Level of Consciousness (the transcendent level)?

4. Among the people you know, think of the person who appears to you to function at the highest Level of Consciousness.

    a. How would you describe him/her as a person?

    b. How would you describe his/her personality?

    c. How would you describe his/her relationships?

    d. How would you describe his/her satisfaction with life?

    e. How does this compare with people you know who function at very low levels of consciousness?

5. What, in your words, is the connection between raising consciousness and expanding the perspectives a person considers in his/her thinking?

6. What connections have you observed between a person's level of objectivity and his/her behavior within relationships?

Consciousness as a Means to Great Relationships

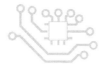

Each Level of Consciousness has various needs and values that are important to it. Within the context of relationships, as you come to understand the "flavor" of each Level of Consciousness, give careful consideration to what that Level of Consciousness considers as being aligned with it. To be viewed by a Level of Consciousness as being aligned with it, you must be seen as supportive toward its desires and values. As discussed earlier, the Instinctual Level of Consciousness focuses on the acquisition of the basic resources necessary to sustain life. In very simplistic terms, at the Instinctual Level of Consciousness, one must continuously be viewed as an aid (if not a source) for providing necessary resources in order to be viewed as being aligned. Fail in this, and that Level of Consciousness will view you as either valueless or hostile.

At the Individualist Level of Consciousness, one must be viewed as a supporter of the individual's ego and security to be aligned. At the Conformist Level of Consciousness, one must be viewed as a member in good standing of the person's "tribe" to be in favor. At the Rational Level, one must typically be viewed as "right" or "in the right" to be aligned. At the Pluralistic Level of Consciousness, one will view all humans as being in some degree of alignment, although that Level of Consciousness will only truly identify with and give its full support to others who are "decent human beings." At the Integral Level and Transcendent Level, all people are viewed as in alignment, and support is readily extended to anyone in need.

Knowing what each Level of Consciousness demands to be considered as being aligned gives one a good idea of the price one will have to pay in order to maintain a good relationship. Without knowing this, one is likely to be confronted with a situation where all that one has invested in the relationship during the good times goes out the window when challenges arise.

A very simplified table, providing an overview of what "price" each Level of Consciousness requires for viewing another person as aligned with it, is as follows:

Aligned Relationships	
Level of Consciousness	*To Be Aligned with a Person Who Is at This Level, You Must*
Instinctual	Be an aid or source for securing necessary resources
Individualist	Be a supporter of the person's ego or security
Conformist	Be a member in good standing of the person's "tribe"
Rational	Be right or "in the right"
Pluralistic	Be a decent human being
Integral	Be a human being
Transcendent	Exist

Table 2. The "price" of alignment with others.

As the table illustrates, the higher the Level of Consciousness at which a person functions, the less needy he or she will be in personal relationships.

There is a "down" side of the coin that needs to be understood in evaluating relationships, namely the probability and consequences of falling out of alignment with that Level of Consciousness. It is important to understand that in any relationship there will be two perspectives. In a different-level relationship, what each will require for alignment will be different from what the other will require. So if person A is functioning at the Pluralistic Level of Consciousness, and person B is functioning at the Integral Level, it is quite possible that person A may view person B as unaligned with him/her, while person B continues to view person A as being aligned with him/her. So in this section, we will focus on the other person's perspective within the relationship.

By looking at the "price" each level requires, it is easy to see that the lower the Level of Consciousness a person is functioning at, the more likely he or she will view another person as being out of alignment. If a partner is functioning at the Individualist Level of Consciousness, all one has to do is fail to support his/her ego or perceived safety needs in order to fall out of alignment (from his/her perspective). Even more challenging to be with a person functioning at the Instinctual Level of Consciousness, one must constantly provide the partner or aid him or her in securing resources in order to remain in alignment. This translates into a very simple but very important rule of thumb: the lower the Level of Consciousness a person is functioning at, the harder he or she will be to keep as a friend.

How Each Level Views Those out of Alignment

At higher Levels of Consciousness, the odds of falling out of alignment with that Level of Consciousness are significantly diminished. In fact, for those functioning within the Harmonic Range of Consciousness (at the Integral or Transcendent Level), merely being alive guarantees that you will remain in alignment with others at this level. While they may not support your actions or your choices or your beliefs, they will readily extend their love to you and support you as a human being.

Secondarily, it is important to have an idea of the ramifications of being out of alignment with the Level of Consciousness involved. As discussed, the focus and concern of the Instinctual Level of Consciousness is acquiring fundamentally needed resources. Without those resources, those functioning at the Instinctual Level will view their welfare, if not their survival, as being in jeopardy. If those functioning at the Instinctual Level of Consciousness view you as being unaligned with them, the probability that they will see you as expendable or as a threat to their welfare or survival is uncomfortably high. That being the case, there is a strong likelihood that their reactions to and behavior toward you will be quite negative and even aggressive. The likelihood of violence, theft, threat, intimidation, and other hostile or "lawless" behavior is not low. As will be discussed later, the morality of this Level of Consciousness justifies and sanctions these actions as appropriate responses to a perceived serious threat. Crossing someone functioning at this Level of Consciousness is a dangerous undertaking.

If people functioning at the Individualist Level of Consciousness view you as being unaligned with them, they will likely see you as being hostile to their security or ego. This is only one step removed from threatening their physical well-being. The odds are good that they will view you as an impediment to their welfare, their welfare being measured by the satisfaction of their egos. In such circumstances, they will likely react to and behave toward you quite negatively, if not with outright hostility. This stance toward you will also most likely be seen as a necessary and appropriate measure of self-protection. This is so because they view their ego as their "self." Frequently, they will feel a need to "vindicate" themselves, which can fester as a seething thirst for vengeance.

If those functioning at the Conformist Level of Consciousness view you as being unaligned with them, they are likely to view you as an "outsider." They will see you as someone who needs to be guarded against or even isolated in order to protect their tribe's interests, codes, or beliefs. Feeling the safety and protection that being a member of the tribe affords them, they are less likely to be physically hostile toward you unless you are viewed as hostile toward and capable of damaging their tribe's interests. However, at this Level of Consciousness, they will likely make efforts to involve others in their disputes with you, and will actively seek to secure allies and turn others against you. Gossip and verbal sabotage are favored mediums and are often vigorously pursued.

If those functioning at the Rational Level of Consciousness view you as being unaligned with them, they will likely see you as being erroneous, primitive, or ignorant. They may criticize you or attempt to "correct," "educate," or "reform" you in a manner they consider "prudent," "just," or "right." However, with development at this level, they will likely realize the possibility that they could be at least partially in error. As the standard of measure at this Level of Consciousness is truth and accuracy, there will likely be some recognition that "truth" is what it is regardless of what kind of defense it receives. Consequently, a self-defensive reaction is less likely to arise and also less likely to be fanned by emotions. While their reaction may be cold and calculating, it probably will not be irrational and explosive as it often is at lower levels.

If people functioning at the Pluralistic Level of Consciousness view you as being unaligned with them, you may well hurt their feelings, but they are unlikely to harbor any actual ill-will toward you. For those functioning at this Level of Consciousness, vengeance is no longer a feasible or useful response. The worst you can likely expect would be for them to end the relationship if it is not worth the trouble it causes them.

As previously discussed, a person functioning within the Harmonic Range of Consciousness (at the Integral Level or the Transcendent Level) will in essence always view you as being in alignment with him or her. However, this is not the same thing as being viewed as an ally or close friend.

In summary, the litmus test for what you can expect in a relationship with a person is, "How does that person treat others who are unaligned with him/her?" Let's assume that Terry and Pat are considering a relationship. Terry asks, "How does Pat treat people whom she views as being unaligned with her?" Because what Pat will do to others, Terry can expect her to someday do to him. Unless Pat is functioning in the Harmonic Range of Consciousness, odds are that there will be times when Pat views Terry as being unaligned with her. And as we have seen from a review of the demands of each Level of Consciousness, the lower the Level of Consciousness Pat is functioning at, the more frequently Terry is likely to be viewed as unaligned and the more extreme Pat's reaction is likely to be.

Also, as will be discussed later, when looking at the Moral Line of Consciousness, it becomes clear that the lower the Level of Consciousness others are functioning at, the greater the likelihood that they will find it acceptable to do you harm, be it physical, emotional, or social. See the simplified table below for possible or even probable reactions to someone viewed as being unaligned.

Unaligned Relationships	
Level of Consciousness	*Possible/Probable Reactions*
Instinctual	Physical attack, threat, intimidation, theft, or property destruction
Individualist	Directly negative or hostile behavior and pursuit of vindication
Conformist	Gossip, slander, and a rally of "allies" with efforts to isolate you
Rational	Criticism or attempts to correct, educate, or justly reform you
Pluralistic	Discussion or avoidance
Integral	No reaction
Transcendent	No reaction

Table 3. Possible to probable individual reactions in each level to other individuals viewed as unaligned.

As the table illustrates, the higher the Level of Consciousness people are functioning at, the less damage they will do in their personal relationships. As consciousness grows, it expands. It takes in, values, and processes more and more perspectives and considerations. It also views a wider and wider circle of people as being in harmony with it. At higher levels, consciousness sees itself as one with the whole world. As psychologists and many schools of metaphysical thought tell us, our minds tend to project our thoughts onto others. We tend to paint other people with the thoughts, motivations, fears, and weaknesses that live within us. We tend to assume that they are acting with the same motives and purposes as we would if we were in their place. Because of this, other people in our lives can often appear as mirrors and reflections of ourselves.

Our Level, Our Mirror

There is a story of a wise mystic who was having a conversation with a surly young man. The young man said to the mystic, "I look at you, and I'm disgusted. You're so full of crap." The mystic smiled and said, "I see. When I look at you I see the divine light of God." The young man was quite taken aback by this response. "How can you say that? Especially considering what I think of you?" The mystic just smiled and said, "When a man's mind is full of the divine light of God, everywhere he looks he sees that divine light. When a man's mind is full of crap, everywhere he looks, crap is what he sees." People who operate at higher levels of consciousness are like the mystic. They have eliminated the "crap" from their minds, and thus from their worlds. (Perception is reality, as far as the mind is concerned.) They are filled with love for every living thing, and when they look upon their world, that is what is reflected back to them. Even a blade of grass can love you once you've learned how to love it.

As we will see from our review of the lines of consciousness, the self-defensive "stuff" is rooted out of our consciousness as it grows up the levels. As the consciousness's identification grows more and more expansive, it recognizes itself as less and less susceptible to harm. If a man believes himself to be his ego, all you have to do is bruise his ego to cause him pain. For a man who has transcended his ego, it is impossible to hurt him by insulting him. In this way, as consciousness grows up the levels, its vulnerabilities diminish. With diminished vulnerabilities, the experience of pain diminishes. With less chance of experiencing pain, the consciousness has less to fear. With less to fear, the consciousness has more room for love and happiness and peace. At the highest levels of consciousness, vulnerability is banished. Fear is banished. Evil is banished. At the highest level, sorrow and pain have passed away. This is the world in which those at the highest levels of consciousness live.

Imagine living in a world where every human being genuinely loves you and values your well-being, a world where chance and fate are your friends and they constantly help you, a world where nothing bad ever happens. This is the world that those at the highest levels of consciousness live in. This is not to say that their cars never get flat tires, that they never get sick or injured, or they never suffer losses. They do. The difference is that they are able to see a bigger picture. And because they are able to see the bigger picture, they understand these things are not bad. As Shakespeare wrote, "Nothing is either good or bad but thinking makes it so."

Many people who have been fired from their jobs find it devastating. And yet many of them, five or ten years later in their life, will tell you it was the best thing that could have happened to them, because if they had not been fired, then this wouldn't have happened and that wouldn't have happened and they wouldn't be where they are now. And where they are now is much better than where they were then. Those at higher levels of consciousness understand this. It is not what happens that is good or bad, it is what we do with it that matters.

The shortest and most effective road to living in a flawless world is to raise our consciousness. By understanding the map of consciousness and frequently contemplating it, we can successfully accomplish two very important things. Both of them are fundamental to our having a high quality of life experience. We can develop better relationships, and we can increase our own happiness.

The Structure (Map) of Consciousness

By focusing on consciousness and learning its traits and structures, we can go below the surface layer that fools and disappoints so many people. We can access and build upon the underlying foundation that will determine how life presents itself to us. Because we have the power to change our Level of Consciousness, we have the power to change our world. And the better we understand the structure of consciousness, the more effective and efficient we will be in making those changes.

Quite simply, in order to live life at the most gratifying levels, we have to work for it. While our right to live such a life is free for the taking, it takes work to learn how to use that gift. It is much like a car. Although we may own it and have a set of keys, that doesn't mean we won't crash it. We have to learn how to drive it and follow the rules of the road in order to get the most out of it. Learning those things takes time and effort.

Understanding the structure of consciousness is like having a road map. The clearer and more detailed the map we have, the better we can find our way. We have already covered the Seven Levels of Consciousness. We will also be looking at three specific "lines" of consciousness. These seven levels and three lines can be thought of as our map of consciousness. They help us understand its structure and organization. If we want to raise our consciousness and improve our experience of life, the map will help guide us there.

Additionally, we will cover the Twenty-One Indices of Consciousness. These are specific skills that people have in varying degrees. They are like driving skills. The better our driving skills, the more likely we are to reach our destination without crashing. Also, having a good understanding of these "driving skills" will help us identify when other drivers are not using them, warning us to keep a safe distance. Furthermore, once we develop them, these driving skills help us to continue driving crash-free.

The first step of our work is to get a good working knowledge of our map and driving skills. This means learning and being familiar with the map of consciousness and the Indices of Consciousness. The second step is to work on developing our driving skills and using them to carry us up the levels of consciousness while being guided by our map.

The third step is the most difficult. As we "drive" through our lives, we will face situations where our knowledge of the map and good driving skills tell us that the way we've always done or viewed something is not taking us where we want to go. While these beliefs or habits are comfortable because they are what we are used to, they either carry us in the wrong direction or cause us to crash. When we recognize that these things are blocking us, we must decide whether or not we are going to change them. Early on, these changes are difficult. They can be frightening or painful or both. But if we are going to improve our experience of life, we must change, and our consciousness must evolve. Having the honesty, strength, and courage to make these changes in ourselves is what separates those who achieve the highest satisfaction in life from those who don't.

Fortunately, these changes get easier as we progress. Having made a change and seen the benefits it brings, it is easier to take on the next change. But the long and the short of it is this: if we want to improve our experience of life, changing ourselves and evolving is how we do it.

Questions for Group or Individual Exploration

1. What are some situations where you have observed people going from being "aligned" to "unaligned." What happened as a result of it?

2. What are some examples you have observed where a person's projecting his or her own thoughts onto someone else, created problems?

3. What are some examples from some of your relationships where your having a different Level of Consciousness from the other person created, or contributed to, stress within the relationship?

4. What are some reasons why people at higher levels of consciousness might be less needy in relationships?

5. In what ways might relationships with people at low levels of consciousness be "riskier" relationships?

6. In what ways might raising consciousness diminish distrust within a relationship?

7. How might sharing the same Level of Consciousness between two people in a relationship improve communication between them?

8. How might using a general map of consciousness be helpful in raising consciousness?

The Roads
Consciousness Travels

In addition to the Seven Levels of Consciousness, there are also *Lines* of Consciousness that are present within each level. As Ken Wilbur points out, there are *lines* of conscious development that develop independently of each other. For example, a person may have excellent cognitive abilities but very poor interpersonal skills. This is the classic archetype of a geek—very bright intellectually but having poor social skills. Intellectual skills would be one Line of Consciousness and interpersonal skills would be another. So, in assessing a person's Level of Consciousness, we need to be aware of which Line of Consciousness we are focusing on. For our purposes, we will focus on Three Lines of Consciousness: the Self-Awareness Line, the Moral Line, and the Interpersonal Line. There are many more Lines of Consciousness, but these have the most direct and universal impact on our experience of happiness.

To look at the relationship between Lines of Consciousness and Levels of Consciousness, let's look at a couple of analogies.

First, let's use elementary school as at metaphor to explain and compare these two different aspects of consciousness. The Seven Levels of Consciousness are much like grade levels 1 through 7. The Lines of Consciousness are like subjects in school, such as language arts, math, and social studies. They have different components and complexities at each of the Seven Levels. Each level of each line serves as a foundation and building block for the next level on that line. Since Lines of Consciousness can (and usually do) develop independently, it is not at all uncommon to find people functioning in one line (subject) at a different level (grade) than they are in another line (subject). This is like a person functioning at the fifth grade level in math but at the second grade level in social studies.

Next, let's also consider our map of consciousness in comparing Lines of Consciousness and Levels of Consciousness. We can think of the Seven Levels as geographic areas, like states in the United States. Lines of Consciousness are like highways running through those states. To get a good idea of where others are functioning consciously, we need to know what highway they are on and which state they are in.

Three Primary Lines of Consciousness

As has been discussed, there are many more than three Lines of Consciousness. But for simplicity's sake, we are going to focus on the three that have the most direct bearing on happiness. They are the main highways that will take us where we want to go.

These three primary lines are the Self-Awareness Line, the Moral Line, and the Interpersonal Line. Intelligence, or cognitive skill, is not the same thing as Consciousness. Intelligence is another Line of Consciousness, but not consciousness itself. A person can be functioning at a very high level of intelligence but at a very low Level of Consciousness.

The Self-Awareness Line.

This Line of Consciousness centers on people's awareness of self and their beliefs, assumptions, and the thoughts and feelings that continuously flow through them. As this line is followed up through the Seven Levels of Consciousness into the higher levels, we develop a clearer sense of who we are, of what motivates us at the deepest levels, and of what our purpose in life is/should be.

The Moral Line.

This Line of Consciousness deals with a person's sense of right and wrong. In the lower Levels of Consciousness, it tends to be rule oriented. As it develops into higher levels, more complex and extensive factors are included in one's evaluations of what is right and wrong. The things that determine the properness of your perspectives and actions and the chain of ramifications that follow from them grow more expansive.

The Interpersonal Line.

This Line of Consciousness deals with our skills and abilities in interacting with other people. At the lower Levels of Consciousness, it centers on following customs of interaction and instinctual drives. At the middle levels, it can be thought of as social skills. At the higher levels, we are better at perceiving and understanding the psyche of others. This enables us to relate to other people in a more effective manner.

The Self-Awareness Line Relative to the Seven Levels of Consciousness

The Self-Awareness Line of Consciousness is arguably the most important. It involves our ability to accurately perceive the subtle forces at play within us. Without recognizing and being aware of these forces, we cannot achieve control over our thoughts, reactions, and actions. If we lack the ability to control our thoughts, reactions, and actions, we have no control over who and what we will become. The Self-Awareness Line centers on our perception of who and what we are. It provides both the foundation and the context within which our reality is drawn.

The Self-Awareness *Line* manifests itself differently depending on our *Level* of Consciousness. (Please recall the Seven Levels already covered: instinctual, individualist, conformist, rational, pluralistic, integral, and transcendent.) At the Instinctual *Level*, awareness of self centers on satisfying the body's physical needs. One is only self-aware in terms of the physical body. The consciousness focuses on factors for insuring one's continued physical existence, as driven by basic human instincts. As such, the consciousness's concern is constantly assessing the need for and availability of the essential things required for the continuation of physical life. Examples are food, water, clothing, shelter, and tools that help the individual acquire and keep those things. It also includes such things as resources that help ensure our physical safety. Others' needs will often go unnoticed, or they may be viewed as threatening to the needs of the individual.

When a person functions at the Individualist Level, he or she perceives self primarily in terms of ego. His or her concept of self extends beyond a mere physical body in the present. The scope of needs that the consciousness contemplates extends a greater distance into the future. It also covers a more expansive and subtle set of threats that it sees itself as needing to guard against. The basic drives of instinct now arise more subtly as the person's emotions. The person sees self as a physical entity that will have needs in the future, and these needs are brought to the conscious forefront, driven by emotion. As such, the concept of self expands into a more abstract dimension, and the individual begins to think of self as more than just a physical presence. Consequently, the consciousness, being now aware of future needs, will strategically compete for resources the individual may not presently need but may need in the future.

At the Conformist Level of Consciousness, an individual begins to perceive relationships as a part of self, in that those relationships are resources that can be drawn on in times of need. In order to assure one's ability to draw on those relationships, one's standing within the tribe becomes important. As a result, the principles of honor, respect, and loyalty arise. The self is now viewed as not only a present physical presence, but also as an actor within a group. The cache of goodwill it carries is viewed as an important part of who it is. As a result of this, a herd mentality often arises. Rather than always acting to satisfy the demands of emotions, the individual's desire to satisfy the expectations of the clan will often prevail.

At the Rational Level of Consciousness (we are still within the Self-Awareness Line), people view themselves as an actor on a much larger stage. The mind's ability to think abstractly and strategically becomes an important part of their identity. Individuals recognize that how they exercise those skills in the present will significantly impact the future and who they become. As a result, these individuals begin to view their thoughts, beliefs, choices, and actions as a part of who they are.

At the Pluralistic Level of Consciousness, we tend to see self as one among other equals whose needs are also important. As our ability to empathize develops, our recognition of the similarities between ourselves and others grows deeper. As such, our concept of self begins to extend beyond our own physical presence, needs, and beliefs. We begin to see familiar parts of ourselves as also being within everyone else. As a result, we develop a sense of seeing ourselves in others. Additionally, we learn to genuinely love ourselves in a healthy way, despite our own flaws and shortcomings. Having learned this, we are able to genuinely love others, warts and all. At this Level of Consciousness, feelings of separateness, isolation, and loneliness begin to lose their foothold in our consciousness.

At the Integral Level of Consciousness, again traveling on the Self-Awareness Line, we recognize self as an integral part within an elegant and harmoniously functioning system called reality. When viewing things from this bigger picture, different perspectives and Levels of Consciousness among people are seen as necessary and positive parts of reality rather than a flaw, annoyance, or challenge. The perception of "flaws" in life and in people gives way to a perception of the beauty of the overall system. As such, the individual views self as a part of and beneficiary from the "system" of life as a whole. At this Level of Consciousness, the individual typically sees himself or herself as an entity that will live beyond this "life."

Finally, at the Transcendent Level of Consciousness, one perceives self as the manifestation of the "divine" that animates all things. Viewing self in this way, the individual identifies with and sees self within all things, and accepts self as an actor within all actions. The line between "self" and "others" becomes so thin as to be in certain contexts, transparent. The being and welfare of all life are viewed as essential parts of who one is.

The following table gives you an at-a-glance summary of the individual's perceptions of "self" at each of the Levels of Consciousness.

The Self-Awareness Line of Consciousness	
Level of Consciousness	*Dominant Perception of "Self"*
Instinctual	A body with immediate needs
Individualist	A body needing to secure its future security
Conformist	A member of a "tribe"
Rational	A being made of a body, thoughts, beliefs, choices, and actions
Pluralistic	One of countless equals, all of whom are important
Integral	An integral piece of a harmonious system of reality
Transcendent	Everything

Table 4. Self-awareness manifests differently depending on one's Level of Consciousness.

The Moral Line Relative to the Seven Levels of Consciousness

The Moral Line of Consciousness centers on our perspective of right and wrong. It can be thought of as the code of ethics we will follow in the absence of external controls. It is one thing for a person not to steal because he is afraid of going to jail if he is caught; it is another if he chooses not to steal because he believes it is wrong. In this example, an individual's morals will determine whether or not he would steal if he could do so with impunity. The Moral Line of Consciousness deals with an individual's self-imposed guidelines of behavior should he find himself in a "gray" area.

At the Instinctual Level of Consciousness, morality centers on the preservation of the individual's life through the acquisition of needed resources and vigorous self-defense. Stealing has no negative moral ramifications for a person functioning at this level because the primary moral imperative is self-preservation. Likewise taking resources from another person by force also violates no moral principles, as again the preservation of life justifies the use of force. Killing in self-defense and even killing to acquire needed resources is justified as the moral dictate is self-preservation; the luxury of concern for others' welfare outside one's closest circle has not yet entered the conscious domain.

At the Individualist Level of Consciousness, moral concerns center on acquiring and maintaining safety by controlling one's environment. This includes those with whom one is in a relationship. The individual is able to perceive and consider less immediate ramifications of his actions. Indiscriminate killing, which was morally dubious at the Instinctual Level of Consciousness, now becomes a potential issue. The future risks to one's own safety that may result from the killing of others now becomes recognizable. One's concerns and actions are governed by what one believes will provide the greatest safety and control. The moral standard for people functioning at this level is whether their conduct will increase, decrease, or maintain their security. People functioning primarily at the Individualist Level of Consciousness will typically attempt to control the people they are in relationships with, as they believe this is how they can best keep themselves, their egos, and their resources secure. People functioning at this level will have no qualms about mistreating someone who is powerless and could not possibly threaten their safety or resources. Moreover, they will be compelled to do others harm if they believe it will increase their own safety in some way.

At the Conformist Level of Consciousness, close relationships take on great significance. The measure of right and wrong is determined by how one's actions affect acceptance within the tribe. Accordingly, the individual may forgo some immediate benefit to self if it will preserve or improve acceptance within the tribe. Likewise, the individual will readily harm others outside the tribe if this will bring tribe approval. The views of the tribe are often and typically "solidified" into a set of rules or customs. As such, the individual may exhibit a near-blind adherence to the rules/customs, even if it results in horrific individual injustice. At this Level of Consciousness, the individual lacks the ability to effectively make his or her own assessment and determination of objective fairness.

At the Rational Level of Consciousness, morality is dictated by logical considerations and centers on objective "truth" and fairness. The group of people whose perspectives the individual is now capable of adopting within the scope of considerations expands considerably. Additionally, the individual is able to logically anticipate the ramifications of his actions—so much so that he is able to perceive and operate based on abstract principles. Justice and fairness become the moral standard, as the individual is now capable of viewing things from the perspective of a "generic" or "neutral" person. The individual now recognizes the principle that the rights he wishes to enjoy must be respected for others. Not wanting to be killed or robbed by any other person, the individual accepts the logical corollary that he should not kill or steal from anyone either.

At the Pluralistic Level of Consciousness, love becomes the moral standard. At this level, egalitarian considerations take hold, and one sees other people in general as equal in worth to oneself. At this level, the moral dictates take on a shift from "do no harm" to affirmatively doing good. One will often choose to help others, even complete strangers, despite the fact that there may be no direct benefit to oneself. Individuals functioning at this level will frequently forgo strict justice in favor of compassion and mercy.

At the Integral Level of Consciousness, the individual's morality centers on the welfare of humanity as a whole. Every human being is given dignity and respect within the scope of the individual's considerations. Actions are taken and decisions are made with a fuller consideration of their extended effects. The individual becomes effective at appropriately tailoring responses to the circumstances that arise. Right and wrong are determined based on what provides the greatest benefit to the greatest number of people over the longest period of time. Individuals functioning at the Integral Level are more effective at discriminating the proper balance between the rights and needs of an individual and the rights and needs of the society of which the individual is a part. Recognizing the intrinsic values (and weaknesses) of various moral approaches, this individual is capable of responding to situations with justice, mercy, or a mix of the two to best address the situation at hand.

At the Transcendent Level of Consciousness, morality takes on a new dimension. The universe is seen as one organic whole, and "right" and "wrong" lose their meaning, as all actions are seen as the universe's interactions with itself. The moral standard centers on the willing utilization of all manifestations of circumstances of "life" as opportunities for evolution. While justice and mercy are not unimportant, the deeper question becomes, "Is growth and evolution of consciousness occurring?"

A table showing the moral dictates of each Level of Consciousness is as follows:

The Moral Line of Consciousness	
Level of Consciousness	*Moral Standard/Dictate*
Instinctual	Self-preservation
Individualist	Acquisition and maintenance of security
Conformist	Approval by the clan
Rational	Justice
Pluralistic	Love
Integral	The greatest good
Transcendent	Evolution

Table 5. The Moral Line as it functions within each of the Seven Levels.

The Interpersonal Line Relative to the Seven Levels of Consciousness

The Interpersonal Line of Consciousness deals with our motives, habits, and methods of interacting with other people. However, it is primarily concerned with the driving force behind why we interact with others. In this Line of Consciousness, it is important to make a determination over an adequate period of time. The fact that we are functioning primarily at the Integral Level of Consciousness does not mean we would never take measures to protect our security, such as installing a home security system or buying insurance, but concerns over safety and the security of property do not regularly occupy the forefront of our thoughts. On the other hand, if we fret day in and day out over what other people think of us, and we feel compelled to try to control others' perceptions, then we are probably functioning at the Individualist Level of Consciousness.

Another important factor to consider with the Interpersonal Line of Consciousness is that there will always be at least two participants in any interpersonal interaction. Quite frequently, the people involved will be at different Levels of Consciousness. The higher the Level of Consciousness a person is functioning at, the more he or she will appear as a chameleon. The reason for this is quite simple. As has already been discussed, a person can use the Level of Consciousness at which he or she primarily functions, as well as all the levels below their primary one. A person cannot function effectively in a Level of Consciousness that he has not yet reached. For example, if a second grader and a seventh grader have a conversation, the seventh grader will have to speak in second grade terms to have a meaningful discussion. If the seventh grader then has a conversation with a fifth grader, the seventh grader can speak in fifth grade terms. As a result, a person functioning at a very high Level of Consciousness could appear to be all over the board, depending on who he is interacting with. To really know for sure, one has to observe a person engaging with people who are at or above his or her Level of Consciousness to figure out where that person truly is.

At the Instinctual Level of Consciousness, relationships are driven by the pursuit of basic essentials for survival. Emotional needs are a luxury that this Level of Consciousness does not have the leisure to pursue. Interaction focuses primarily on what resources can be obtained through that interaction. The fairness and impact the interaction has on the other person is of little concern, unless that person is seen as a potential ongoing source of necessities. Once a person ceases to be a resource for satisfying essential needs, their importance is negligible, except for their potential as a threat. When actual or perceived conflict arises, the reaction can often be aggressive, hostile, and violent.

At the Individualist Level of Consciousness, interpersonal interaction focuses on acquiring and maintaining security. For our purposes here, security includes not only physical safety, but also the protection of property and interests. In terms of emotional needs, this Level of Consciousness seeks to be recognized and validated in virtually all that it does. Most people view this as excessive insecurity. Control is viewed as the most reliable method of ensuring the safety and advancement of the ego. Interaction often involves ongoing efforts to control others. On the most basic level, this means efforts at controlling others' behaviors—even by force, if it can be exercised without retribution. Great attention and effort are devoted to limiting others' actions that are seen as potentially threatening to the person's security and pressing for actions that are seen as supportive of the person's security. In a more abstract, intellectual realm, it includes efforts to control other people's perceptions of the individual. This ensures that the individual is viewed by others in the way he wishes to be seen. Those functioning at this Level of Consciousness believe that the best way to control others' behaviors toward them is to control what those people think about them. Furthermore, people who think well of them are more likely to affirm and validate them, satisfying their emotional needs. When actual or perceived conflict arises, the other person is viewed as a threat and is typically reacted to quite negatively.

At the Conformist Level of Consciousness, interpersonal interactions are guided by reference to the customs and values of the tribe. Interactions often center on the benefits they accrue for the tribe as well as the individual. Much energy is devoted to determining other people's level of identification with and conformance to the tribe's culture. Individuals at this level want to know whether other people are on their team or not. There will often be efforts aimed at "converting" or "proselytizing" those who aren't. In terms of emotional needs, this Level of Consciousness seeks acceptance and a sense of belonging. Individuals will, at times, pursue benefits for people other than themselves. This is especially true if it will benefit an important member of the clan. Interactions and discussions frequently center on individual people—what they think, what they've said, and what they've done. When an actual or perceived conflict arises, the reaction often focuses on portraying the other individual as a traitor or as evil, and efforts are made to highlight how the offending individual is in violation of clan standards and thereby villainous. This behavior is often accompanied by efforts to rally allies to the "innocent" individual's side and to actively turn people against the offending individual.

At the Rational Level of Consciousness, interpersonal interactions typically center on concepts and ideas. The dominant emotional need at this level is for intellectual stimulation and the pursuit and discovery of "truth" or pragmatically useful information. As the focus of discussion, ideas will typically take center stage over the discussion of individual people. When actual or perceived conflict arises, the other individual is typically viewed as "wrong" or in error. Efforts are often then made to prove this. However, someone who is truly functioning at the intellectual level will criticize the idea or the argument rather than the person who raised it.

At the Pluralistic Level of Consciousness, interpersonal interactions take into account the benefits they provide to both people involved. Emotionally, the dominant need is genuine love. The "I love you because you fill my needs" version of "love" is no longer satisfactory for this Level of Consciousness. Having developed an understanding that true love comes as an unconditional gift, and not a need in disguise, those at this level seek the real thing. The most satisfying interactions are those that qualify as "win–win." Charity arises as a valued practice for its own sake, rather than for the benefits it will secure for the individual who extends it. People functioning at this Level of Consciousness will extend courtesy and respect to everyone, including those who are in the wrong, outsiders, and even enemies. When actual or perceived conflict arises, efforts are often made at reconciliation or the extension of compassion. Vengeance is no longer viewed as an acceptable personal response. Where appropriate, those at this Level of Consciousness have no problem in offering an apology or accepting responsibility for something they didn't do, if it will lead to a positive and healthy resolution. Those who are viewed as being in error are typically viewed not as evil, but merely as being in a state of lacking adequate information or understanding, a personal circumstance rather than a character or intellectual flaw.

At the Integral Level of Consciousness, interpersonal interactions focus on benefiting society and its individuals, and diversity itself is valued. In terms of emotional needs, this Level of Consciousness seeks the satisfaction of having made a positive contribution to society. When actual or perceived conflict arises, it is viewed as merely different perspectives of the same phenomenon, with each perspective having its own strengths and weaknesses. As such, conflict resolution frequently focuses on addressing the core issue, rather than "fixing" the individuals who hold the divergent points of view. The parties can agree to disagree and still arrive at constructive forward progress on the challenge at hand.

At the Transcendent Level of Consciousness, interpersonal interactions focus on the advancement of all of life. While the individuals involved are important aspects, they are viewed as various manifestations of the same underlying reality. Issues that, at other levels of consciousness, would be perceived as conflict are here viewed as a natural and healthy part of the process of universal evolution. At this level, the person typically has transcended what most people consider emotional needs. These individuals do what they do, not to satisfy their own needs, but to creatively express the divine light within them.

A summary table showing the predominant motivator for interpersonal interaction based on the person's Level of Consciousness is as follows:

The Interpersonal Line of Consciousness	
Level of Consciousness	*Primary Motivator for Interaction*
Instinctual	Resource acquisition
Individualist	Control and affirmation
Conformist	Acceptance and a sense of belonging
Rational	Intellectual stimulation, truth, and pragmatically useful information
Pluralistic	Genuine love and mutual benefits
Integral	Making a contribution to society
Transcendent	The advancement and benefit of life

Table 6. The Interpersonal Line as it functions within each of the Seven Levels.

Questions for Group or Individual Exploration

1. How would you describe the general differences between (1) the Lines and Levels of Consciousness and (2) the Indices of Consciousness?

2. Why might the Self-Awareness Line of Consciousness be the most influential line of consciousness?

3. What are some examples you have observed in which a person's actions clearly reflected the Level of Consciousness at which he or she was primarily functioning?

4. What are some examples you have observed where people's moral Level of Consciousness was strongly influenced by their circumstances?

5. In what ways would you expect having a relationship with a person functioning primarily at a high Level of Consciousness to be different from having a relationship with a person functioning primarily at a low Level of Consciousness?

6. In your own words, how would you say raising consciousness might contribute to better relationships?

Consciousness as a Powerhouse for Achieving Success in Life

While the lines and levels of consciousness are a nice, neat, simplified way of explaining some of the major patterns and evolution of functioning within the human mind, questions remain: "Are they useful paradigms? What evidence do we have that higher levels of consciousness actually improve our experience of life?" Through the course of my life, I have read and studied hundreds of books in fields as diverse as psychology, religion, spirituality, politics, sociology, and physics. I also worked as a family lawyer for eleven years. Family law is a giant, virtual test tube for observing everything that can go wrong in relationships. It is also a great venue for observing the collision of individual interests with the collective interests of the state. Through all of my studies and all of my experiences, I have observed consciousness as the common actor in many interesting roles. I also observed that the people who truly excelled, who found their way to very happy and fulfilling lives, were the ones who had learned how to consistently function at high levels of consciousness. All of the evidence indicates to me that when we really look at life, the single biggest predictor of the amount of happiness and fulfillment we will experience in life is the Level of Consciousness at which we function.

I believe all of us intuitively know this on some level, but I wanted to test this theory, so I assembled a focus group and surveyed them extensively. I made inquiries to ascertain what Level of Consciousness they would most resonate with in a variety of life situations. I also asked them how happy they were with eighteen different areas of their lives. The results of the informal survey surprised me. The correlation was even stronger than I had expected. First, the seven levels of consciousness were stretched over a 100-point scale. Then, each respondent's level of happiness with fifteen of eighteen areas of their life were averaged together and scaled on a 100-point scale. Amazingly, the respondent's level of happiness was, on average, within nine points of the Level of Consciousness at which he or she primarily functioned. While I was astounded by the results of this survey, it was still informal. It was nowhere near meeting the rigorous requirements required to have any real scientific statistical validity. But it did give me one more data point to work with, and that data appeared consistent with implications drawn from the correlation of many diverse schools of thought tangentially related to consciousness.

As the foundation to his formulation of the hierarchy of needs, Dr. Maslow drew from his many years of work as a psychologist, studying hundreds of people. When we consider the Seven Levels of Consciousness and compare them to Maslow's hierarchy of needs, the overlap is obvious. With just a little stretching, we can

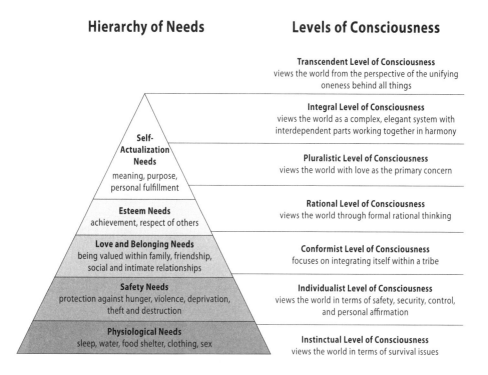

Hierarchy of Needs

Levels of Consciousness

Transcendent Level of Consciousness
views the world from the perspective of the unifying oneness behind all things

Integral Level of Consciousness
views the world as a complex, elegant system with interdependent parts working together in harmony

Self-Actualization Needs
meaning, purpose, personal fulfillment

Pluralistic Level of Consciousness
views the world with love as the primary concern

Esteem Needs
achievement, respect of others

Rational Level of Consciousness
views the world through formal rational thinking

Love and Belonging Needs
being valued within family, friendship, social and intimate relationships

Conformist Level of Consciousness
focuses on integrating itself within a tribe

Safety Needs
protection against hunger, violence, deprivation, theft and destruction

Individualist Level of Consciousness
views the world in terms of safety, security, control, and personal affirmation

Physiological Needs
sleep, water, food shelter, clothing, sex

Instinctual Level of Consciousness
views the world in terms of survival issues

Fig. 4. Maslow's Hierarchy[34] relative to the Seven Levels of Consciousness.

overlay the hierarchy of needs harmoniously on top of the levels of consciousness, as shown in figure 4.

Clearly, Dr. Maslow recognized an organization in the human psyche that has been observed by visionaries the world over. At the pinnacle of Dr. Maslow's hierarchy is the human need for self-actualization. Dr. Maslow famously used the term "self-actualization" to refer to periods in individuals' lives during which they are living at the height of their capacity as human beings, using the fullest expression of their talents, interests, and abilities. Dr. Maslow asserted that peak experiences are times when people have their most profound experiences and insights; during peak experiences, people are essentially at the happiest, most fulfilling points in their lives. Fully matured and self-actualized people have many peak experiences. They live during those periods as the fullest expression of who they are, maximizing their potential and their joy. After self-actualization, Dr. Maslow said, people enter a stage of transcendence in which they begin to focus on helping others attain self-actualization.[35]

When we look at the overlay of Dr. Maslow's hierarchy of needs on top of the levels of consciousness, it becomes clear that what he refers to as self-actualization is when a person is functioning at the higher levels of consciousness. For Dr. Maslow, the evidence was clear that this produced people's greatest, happiest, and most profound experiences in life. This conclusion is echoed in less obvious terms across many fields of thought.

Another set of extensive research also implies that higher levels of consciousness are potentially one of the greatest contributors to a person's professional success. In *The Millionaire*

Mind, Dr. Thomas J. Stanley summarized his conclusions from his extensive surveying and studying of 733 millionaires, in efforts to determine what accounted for their success. He wrote:

> After studying millionaires for more than 20 years, I have concluded that if you can make one major decision correctly, you can become economically productive. If you are creative enough to select the ideal vocation, you can win, win big-time. The really brilliant millionaires are those who selected a vocation that they love, one that has few competitors but generates high profits.[36]

Loving their vocation was one of the three primary factors Dr. Stanley found as being key to choosing a vocation that best supported an individual's financial success. When Dr. Stanley asked the millionaires to list the top thirty factors that most contributed to their success, loving their career/business was number six in the list of thirty. Here are the top six:

1. Being honest with all people.

2. Being well disciplined.

3. Getting along with people.

4. Having a supportive spouse.

5 Working harder than most people.

6. Loving my career/business.

Dr. Stanley says that millionaires with "high creative intelligence often make one very important career decision correctly: They select a vocation that provides them with enormous profits, and very often this same vocation is one they love."[37] Productivity is much higher, says Dr. Stanley, and "creative genius will emerge" when you love your occupation. Stanley also cites the work of Professor Robert J. Sternberg, describing Sternberg as "one of America's leading authorities on human intelligence."[38] According to Stanley, Sternberg says that creative people often succeed because of their love for their chosen profession. "Creative intelligence is a major component of Sternberg's definition of successful intelligence,"[39] says Stanley.

He also says other forms of intelligence don't fare as well:

> Analytically intelligent people often select vocations that are filled with competitors and discover that they don't love their careers. Even if they are geniuses, it's hard to win a competitive economic battle if your heart and emotions are not completely dedicated to victory.[40]

The essential key Dr. Stanley points to for finding a career a person will love is in selecting one that is harmonious with and advances the deepest core interests and motivations of the individual. It is not a matter of falling in love with whatever career one lands in. In fact, Dr. Stanley found that many millionaires had experienced unrewarding or unpleasant work experiences prior to selecting the career that they loved and ultimately became so successful in. In probing for how they made the key selection that set up or enabled their success, Dr. Stanley found that over 80 percent chose their vocation because it allowed "full use of . . . [their] abilities and aptitudes."[41]

Interestingly, their reason for choosing their vocation is strikingly similar to Dr. Maslow's description of self-actualization. These successful people used higher levels of consciousness to access a deep awareness of themselves. This awareness enabled them to formulate an exceptionally effective means of evaluating potential careers. The selections they thus made provided a wonderful compound benefit; the choices allowed them to work at a career they loved, one in which they also were able to become quite financially successful.

Higher consciousness has shown itself capable of making significant contributions to professional and financial success in many ways, some more obvious than others. But of equal significance, higher consciousness contributes to the quality of our inner life as well. When we overlay the hierarchy of needs on the Levels of Consciousness and consider the "background energy" or "background environment" in the psyche that animates the various levels of consciousness, a subtle picture comes into clearer focus. At the lower Levels of Consciousness, we are driven by more primal drives. These primal drives tend to be more brutal on ourselves as well as others. At the lowest Level of Consciousness, the Instinctual Level, these forces are the physically strongest. In a life-or-death situation, adrenaline is pumped into the bloodstream, and the entire body is amped up in the fight-or-flight response. Additionally, the perceived need for control is typically perceived as a critical matter. Our animal/chemical system is flooded with four-alarm energy as we face one do-or-die scenario after another. But as consciousness moves up through the levels, it views fewer and fewer things as threats to its welfare. As we ascend to higher levels of consciousness, the "background energy" in our psyches becomes much more subtle and sublime. The things that each successive Level of Consciousness places the greatest value upon fall less and less outside of its control.

In light of this, we see the "environment of the psyche" in which consciousness functions, varying across the levels of consciousness. This subtle background predisposition of the mind colors how the mind perceives and interprets the events, people, and information it experiences. This relationship of influence is shown in figure 5.

At the lower Levels of Consciousness, the primary background from which the mind forms its perceptions is composed of fear, anger, and a lack of control. These forces diminish as consciousness moves up through the levels and transforms into their polar opposites. Fear subsides and is replaced by peace. Anger is banished, and compassion springs up in its place. The need for control gives way to a desire to serve others. We see these forces rather consistently displayed in the personalities of notable figures. How many persons who were revered as saints did not possess a notable degree of peace, compassion, and service that distinguished them from others? Of the most destructive tyrants in history, were any lacking in anger, a thirst to control others, or a morbid fear of losing their power?

When we set aside the personalities and actions of people who have displayed these traits to significant degrees, we are still left with the inner environment in which they lived. At the lower levels of consciousness, people are constantly hounded by fear, anger, and a strong feeling of insecurity because they feel they lack adequate control over their circumstances. Needless to say, these feelings take

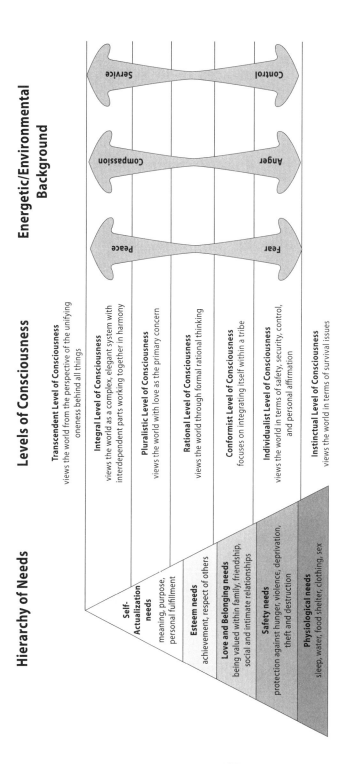

Fig. 5. Maslow's Hierarchy, the Seven Levels of Consciousness, and the Energetic/Environmental Mental Background.

an emotional toll and can eventually take a physical toll as well. Quite obviously, they are a much less pleasant backdrop than are peace, compassion, and a sense of being a benefit to others. Is it any wonder that people who live at higher levels of consciousness have a much more pleasant and fulfilling experience of life?

Questions for Group or Individual Exploration

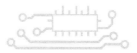

1. What do you see as the similarities between the Levels of Consciousness and Maslow's Hierarchy of Needs?

2. What do you see as the differences between the Levels of Consciousness and Maslow's Hierarchy of Needs?

3. At this point in your life, what would self-actualization look like for you?

4. Does your career offer you the opportunity to make full use of your abilities and aptitudes? If not, what would need to change for that to be the case?

5. What energetic/environmental mental background pre-dominates in your psyche? Why do you think that is the case? Is it presently how you want it to be? If not, what do you see as your greatest leverage point for making it what you would like for it to be?

The Twenty-One Indices
of Consciousness

Having reviewed the structure and significance of consciousness, let us now consider the practical side. How does this skill of consciousness apply itself in our everyday lives? What are some tools and checklists we can use in sharpening our skill? Within this paradigm of consciousness, the insights, research, and conclusions of some of the most famous and illumined minds in human history figure prominently. Various concepts tend to emerge again and again in wisdom schools, spiritual traditions, religions, philosophies, and even psychology as key ingredients to a higher consciousness. The Twenty-One Indices of Consciousness represents a distilled list that expresses those ideas. They are arguably the top twenty-one facets of higher consciousness that have regularly and routinely surfaced in human thinking to date:

1. Honesty
2. Egalitarianism
3. Equanimity
4. Faith
5. Responsibility
6. Balance
7. Empathy
8. Nonjudgmentalism
9. Open-mindedness
10. Presentness
11. Courage
12. Appreciation
13. Love
14. Emotional Discipline
15. Mental Discipline
16. Flexibility
17. Positiveness
18. Assertiveness
19. Objectivity
20. Communication
21. Awareness

These Indices can help in deciphering at what general Level of Consciousness individuals are functioning. The more Indices in which they are functioning at the underdeveloped aspect, the lower their Level of Consciousness will be. Conversely, the more Indices they are functioning well in, the higher their Level of Consciousness will be. If you observe a person functioning well in almost all of these Indices, you can feel confident that he or she is living at a very high Level of Consciousness.

Each of the Indices of Consciousness is like a skill that we can, through development, use to make our lives happier. Unlike Lines of Consciousness, which develop independently, the Indices of Consciousness function interdependently and have an influence on each other. They are like pistons in an engine: the greatest performance is achieved when all the pistons (Indices) are functioning together harmoniously. Such harmonious functioning produces a synergistic effect in which the unified whole is greater than the sum of the parts. These Indices serve as the buttons and levers through which we can tune our navigation system (mind) and increase its coherence and power.

As just one example of the power of these Indices, let us consider Egalitarianism. Egalitarianism is the view that all people are of equal worth and dignity. While this is held as a moral or ethical principle by some, it is much more than that. It is a VERY useful way of viewing the world. Without an egalitarian view to serve as an anchor for our thinking, the mind tends to drift into some turbulent waters. Without an egalitarian view, the premise arises that some people are better than others. We are not talking about better in terms of skills or abilities; we are talking about better in terms of their value as a human being. As a natural result, people begin to value other people, determining that some are better than others, and some are worse than others. People who wrong them are immediate candidates for the "worse than" category. Conversely, people who exhibit traits or accomplishments they are impressed with are candidates for the "better than" category. From this thinking, the person then proceeds, quite naturally, to measure himself or herself against others. While it may be understated or even subconscious depending on the level of awareness the person is functioning at, the comparative valuation is continuously going on as the brain constantly sizes up its environment and the people in it.

Inevitably, individuals come to the question of how they stack up against others. Am I better? Am I worse? The ego quite naturally wants to be better, because better means higher odds of getting what it wants. And so a person with a strong ego will often slant the measurement in his own favor, again usually in either an understated manner or subconsciously. As this process progresses and becomes reinforced in subconscious patterns of comparative evaluation, the person develops an inflated sense of self-worth relative to other people. The natural outgrowths of this are conceit, vanity, arrogance, a dismissive attitude toward other people's good qualities, and an inflated sense of other's flaws. We all know the social cost that vanity and arrogance carry with them. Few people like having people with these mindsets as friends. But more subtle is the person's distorted sense of reality as he or she loses the ability to accurately hear information that relates to himself/herself. He is much more likely to "kill the messenger" than actually hear that he or she has real weaknesses that could be improved upon. And without improving upon weaknesses, this person will lose all the benefits that could bring.

On the other side of the equation are people with weak self-esteem. When they measure themselves against others, they tend to focus on their own faults and shortcomings. As the mind gets trained in this pattern of thinking, individuals will find themselves coming up short in most measurements they take. There are always other people to be found who are better looking, smarter, more socially savvy, more impeccably credentialed, or more morally respectable. In the minds of those with low self-esteem, there is always some way in which they fall short of perfection, acceptable standards, or even their own aspirations. The ultimate effect is an ongoing experience of self-flagellation. Anyone who has ever suffered from poor self-esteem can testify to the enormous amounts of mental and emotional energy that it sucks from their life. All the while, the energy it is sucking out of their life could have been spent instead on things that would actually increase their happiness.

Both of these deviations off the centerline of balance that an egalitarian view subconsciously undergirds can carry major costs in terms of mental and emotional energy. They can even carry considerable social and personal growth costs as well. Thus, holding this one perspective can have a huge practical effect on us and our lives. In a similar fashion, each of the Indices of Consciousness serves as a quick and ready boon that pays far-reaching dividends in how our minds think and process energy.

Thousands of years of hard-earned human insight and wisdom have been recorded, compiled, and distilled into a concentrated body of knowledge through the painstaking efforts of many great thinkers and visionaries. So many have lovingly offered their combined wisdom to aid us in our journey to higher consciousness. If a person wants to raise his or her Level of Consciousness, the Indices of Consciousness provide a superb checklist for evaluating and modifying beliefs, values, reactions, and actions. Choosing to and acting consistently with the developed aspect of one of the Indices and avoiding the underdeveloped aspect will, over time, give one mastery of it. By frequently thinking through the Indices and honestly comparing them against how we actually believe, act, and react, we can make this treasure trove of insight and understanding a part of who we are. When we think them through in the context of the Map of Consciousness, we can develop a good understanding of how we are doing in terms of our consciousness. If we can master these indices one by one, we will steadily progress up the Levels of Consciousness.

Honesty

Perhaps the most important, and at times painful, of the indices is **honesty**. Honesty is the commitment we have to see, accept, and speak the truth. When this trait is underdeveloped, dishonesty is seen as a legitimate means to achieve desired ends. Additionally, we have a difficult time in being honest with ourselves about ourselves. Needless to say, this can be a significant inhibitor to growth. As this trait develops, the use of dishonesty with those who we view as being aligned with us is less frequent. However, as can be said with most things, if we are dishonest with those with whom we are unaligned, we will likely be dishonest, though less frequently so, with those who are in alignment with us. When this trait is fully developed, we will strive to be honest with ourselves no matter how painful it might be, and we will be honest with all other people.

Although admitting to and accepting the shadow aspects of ourselves can be very painful, it is absolutely essential to our conscious growth. Without recognizing, acknowledging, and facing our fears and demons, we can never overcome them, and they will continue to haunt and torment us in the background of our minds. Moreover, all the mental territory beyond them will remain hidden to us. Dishonesty, therefore, acts as an effective barrier to a deeper understanding of ourselves and others.

Egalitarianism

The next of the indices is **egalitarianism**. Egalitarianism is the valuation of all people as equal in worth, irrespective of abilities, achievements, or failures. When this trait is underdeveloped, we will constantly weigh one person against another. The measurement goes beyond the mere assessment and calibration of respective skills and becomes a comparison of personhood in which one person is seen as a better or worse person than another. When these value comparisons are exercised with a self-indulgent slant, the ego is inflated. When exercised with a bias toward self-deprecation, self-esteem suffers. When this trait is functioning effectively, we will view all people as equal in worth and as deserving of dignity and respect.

So often in life we see people who do not function well in this index. Many of them, wanting to believe they are better than others, constantly look for ways to criticize and undermine other people. They seek and find all kinds of reasons and justifications why they are superior to others. In extreme cases, this mentality can become institutionalized, such as in the caste system of India or the racism of the Nazis. People in this mindset often suffer from an overinflated and unrealistic view of their skills or contributions.

We also see people at the other extreme who do not view themselves as worthy human beings. Such a view can emerge as a result of neglect or abuse as a child, guilt over something in the past, societal conditioning, or a myriad of other reasons. Such people suffer from low self-esteem and find difficulty justifying their worth because it is sought in something other than their humanity. In skills there will always be someone better. In looks, there will always be someone more attractive. In intelligence, there will always be someone brighter. This is not to say people who excel in skill, effort, intellect, or other talents should not be recognized and rewarded. But those are all products that arise out of what truly makes us valuable—being living human beings.

Equanimity

The next of the indices is **equanimity**. Equanimity is an equal-minded acceptance of all circumstances and the recognition of the intrinsic value of all things. When this trait is underdeveloped, every event and circumstance will be judged as good or bad. Strong preferences will be lodged in favor of certain circumstances and material things or opinions and reactions from other people. When this trait is functioning effectively, we will receive with equal-minded acceptance both easy circumstances and difficult ones. This is not to say we are indifferent and would be just as inclined to walk in front of a bus as wait for it to pass, but when we have exercised what reasonable control we have, we accept the things we cannot control. Likewise, when this trait is functioning effectively, other people's actions and treatment of us will be viewed with a similar even-mindedness. An insult and flattery will have the same non-effect on us.

Those who are not functioning effectively in this trait frequently get caught up in how things ought to or should have happened. Oftentimes, an event will occur that is not in line with what they think should happen, and they experience significant anxiety, anger, or frustration as a result. This reaction can become ingrained and elevated to the point at which their frustration causes them significantly more emotional pain than the actual event itself. This failure of reality to meet their expectations, when repeated over and over, can lead them to respond to life with deep resentment or dejected withdrawal. Rather than loosen their expectations of reality, they condemn reality for not conforming itself to their wishes.

Faith

The next of the indices is **faith**. Faith is the ability to be confident that events and circumstances contain within them opportunities for the betterment of the individual. When this trait is underdeveloped, we live in constant anxiety about what is going to occur or not occur in our lives. We harbor the belief that if we are not in control, the outcome will, at the least, not benefit us and quite likely will be bad for us. When this trait is functioning effectively, we are able to confidently trust that whatever comes to pass will have opportunities for our benefit, be able to recognize those opportunities, capitalize on them, and be appreciative of them.

I can't count the number of people I've heard say something like this: "You know when I got fired (or laid-off) a few years ago, I thought it was the worst thing that could have happened to me. But now when I look back, I realize if that had not happened, then such and such wouldn't have happened, and I wouldn't be where I am now . . . and where I am now is a much better place." People with strong faith are able to believe that when the bump in the road occurs, it will lead them to a better place. As a result, they are able to see as opportunities those events that others see as disasters. Imagine the difference in impact on their stress level!

Responsibility

The next of the indices is **responsibility**. Responsibility is the willingness, ability, and actuality of people's accepting their role in the positive and negative consequences that flow from their actions and inactions. When this trait is underdeveloped, we will try to blame less-than-optimal circumstances in which we are involved on other people, events . . . anything other than ourselves. We are reluctant to accept labors, challenges, and obligations that rightly fall to us. Additionally, we look with disfavor upon being held accountable for what we do or don't do. When this trait is functioning effectively, we will readily take on challenges and labors that are appropriate for us to take. We will accept the blame and the obligation to effect repairs, improvements, or amends if we have contributed to less than ideal circumstances. Further, we have no qualms about being held accountable for our actions and decisions.

Making excuses for personal weaknesses or things that go wrong only makes us look weaker. We're all familiar with people who make excuses for everything. How many of them do we consider reliable? In a company several years ago, there was a major goof on one of the projects. Several people on the team were responsible for completing the project. Top management wanted to know who was responsible for the costly error. While no one was really in charge of the team, Tom identified himself as responsible for the error and got a butt chewing for it. A year and a half later, Tom was promoted over everyone else who had been on the team. One of the other team members asked an upper manager why Tom was the one who got promoted. The manager said, "Because Tom took responsibility for what went wrong, we knew who to talk to to make sure things improved, and we knew who to hold accountable if they didn't. Tom took our advice, and when results improved, we knew who was responsible for it. And when Tom told us things were going well, we knew we could believe him. When he stood up and took the heat in a firestorm, we knew he could handle the calmer waters."

Balance

The next of the indices is **balance**. Balance is the ability to pursue moderation while avoiding extremes; it is the judicious harmonizing of opposites. When this trait is underdeveloped, the person will pursue or be drawn into extremities of view, belief, or action. This can also manifest as overindulgence or addictive behavior. The addict's world tends to be divided into polar opposites, and he or she typically either devotes allegiance to one pole and harbors an aversion to the other, or swings between the extremes, often with chaotic results. When this trait is functioning effectively, the person will balance or blend traits of apparent polar opposites. Many wisdom traditions hold that the path of individual evolution is the process of balancing the masculine and feminine energies within each person. Justice and compassion, convention and innovation, strength and flexibility, and principle and pragmatism are just a few additional examples of dualities that people are constantly striving to balance and harmonize.

Empathy

The next of the indices is **empathy**. Empathy is the ability to place oneself in another's position and see and feel things from the other's perspective. When this trait is underdeveloped, we think of things only from our own point of view and how it impacts us. In extreme cases, we can exact physical cruelty and pain on animals or even other people with no apprehension or concern regarding the pain or damage we are causing. In less extreme cases, while

we may be generally aware of how things will affect others physically, we are oblivious to others' thoughts and feelings outside
what we are told. Even then it can be very difficult for us to truly
understand, respect, or even appreciate them. When this trait is
functioning effectively, we can easily and with a good degree of
accuracy perceive the thoughts and feelings another person may
be experiencing at any given time. Moreover, we respect the other
person's perspective and feelings and can often sense and feel any
emotional pain the other person may be having.

Nonjudgmentalism

The next of the indices is **nonjudgmentalism**. Nonjudgmentalism is the ability and practice of not making conclusory judgments
about people based on their thoughts, beliefs, motives, or actions.
When this trait is underdeveloped, we will readily adopt critical
conclusions and opinions of other people. We will find fault in the
thoughts, actions, and beliefs of others and will readily assume and
assign ill motives to them. Moreover, we will exhibit an inability to
distinguish between a behavior and a person, believing or assuming
that what we see as bad behavior makes the person who engaged
in that behavior bad. When this trait is functioning effectively, we
decline to find fault in others and accept ignorance, mistakes, and
less than perfect thinking, beliefs, and actions as a normal and understandable part of human life that everyone struggles with. Moreover,
we are usually the first to admit that, at some time in our lives, we
have made similar mistakes or could make a similar mistake if we
had the same past or were placed in the same circumstances as the

other person. This is not to say that we decouple and refuse to apply appropriate consequences to inappropriate or illegal behaviors, but we will do so without vilifying the other person. We have no difficulty distinguishing between bad behavior and the person, and recognizing that bad behavior does not, in and of itself, prove a bad person.

The list of judgments people can levy on each other is endless. We might judge others over height, weight, personality, habits, temperament, or any other facet of being human. Many Eastern philosophies discuss the importance of recognizing maya, or the illusory aspect of reality. Judgments are the most common element in the world of maya. When we make judgments, we make conclusory assumptions and view them as though they are true. When we judge a person for his or her actions, we make assumptions about that person's motives. Ninety percent of the time we are wrong. We typically know significantly less than the whole story. So our judgments are merely approximations of reality and not reality itself. Those who doubt this need only review their own response to other people's judgments of them.

Once we make judgments about a person, we then tend to think and believe that our conclusion is how the person actually is. As we layer judgment upon judgment on others, we remove ourselves from truly perceiving them. It is much like taking a picture of a person, photocopying the picture, copying the copy several times, and believing that the last copy is actually the person.

Many times, significant aspects of the other person (frequently the better ones) become hidden to us because of our judgments. This diminishes our capacity to accurately perceive reality as it is. It also populates our world with people who are full of our worst attributes because those attributes are the ones we tend to project onto others when we make judgments about them. When this index is underdeveloped, we tend to assume the worst about people, and we tend to subconsciously use ourselves as a reference for their probable motives. I've always found it interesting that it tends to be the liars who are most worried about being lied to. It also seemed to be the guys who took advantage of the most young ladies in high school and college that were, later in life, the most suspicious of the motives of their daughters' suitors.

Open-Mindedness

The next of the indices is **open-mindedness**. Open-mindedness is the ability to consider new and different ideas, perspectives, and ways of thinking. When this trait is underdeveloped, we feel annoyed or even threatened by any ideas, perspectives, or experiences that are new to us. We view with suspicion anything that is different from what we are used to or accept as "the norm." Change and growth can prove quite difficult for us. When this trait is functioning effectively, we experience no discomfort at exploring new ideas, concepts, and approaches. Although we may not adopt them as our own, we will readily give them our due consideration. Moreover, we are comfortable with people holding belief systems that are different from our own, and we can easily accept that those things may hold validity and benefit for others, even if not for ourselves.

In addition to the interpersonal and intellectual growth benefits, being open-minded significantly increases creative potential.

Just as closed-mindedness tends to cling to the known, the certain, and the conventional, creativity seeks new and original ways of thinking and expressing. Being open to new ways of viewing or expressing thoughts or ideas opens the gate through which creativity can enter. The open mind is also more comfortable with and more likely to generate or perceive new and innovative solutions to problems that would be insurmountable obstacles to more closed-minded thinkers.

Presentness

The next of the indices is **presentness**. Presentness is the ability to remain focused and centered in the here and now. When this trait is underdeveloped, we are constantly preoccupied with "living in" or focusing on the past or the future. Past mistakes, misfortunes, or wrongs suffered are dwelt upon and repeatedly dredged up. Alternatively, we may be consumed with what will, might or should happen in the future. When this trait is functioning effectively, we will remain centered in and focused on the present. This is not to say we neither think of or learn from the past nor plan for the future. Rather, we give them the consideration they are due and then return to the present, making the most of what is in our here and now.

Courage

The next of the indices is **courage**. In the context of the consciousness paradigm, courage is the ability to view fear and emotional pain as being helpful markers for where we have the greatest opportunity for growth and then to actively pursue that growth. When this trait is underdeveloped, we will go to great lengths to avoid difficult or uncomfortable circumstances. We will forgo growth and personal improvement rather than face and deal with pain, emotional discomfort, or our own personal weaknesses or demons. When this trait is functioning effectively, we will recognize fears, pains, and demons as personal weaknesses that need to be dealt with to break their hold and detrimental impact on us. We will readily and honestly own up to, face, and deal with our fears, pains, and discomforts rather than avoid them.

Appreciation

The next of the indices is **appreciation**. Appreciation is the ability to find beauty and value in all things. When this trait is underdeveloped, we will exhibit a lack of gratitude for things that are done for us, even in the greatest cases of charity. We fail to see the inherent beauty and value that exist in things. Instead of counting our blessings, we will fret over all the things that are not to our liking. We also exhibit indifference or even disrespect to the people and things in our lives. When this trait is functioning effectively, we will exhibit respect and gratitude toward everything within our experience. We constantly perceive the intrinsic value in all things and people. We do not take things or people for granted, and we feel a sincere sense of gratitude for all that we receive and for the opportunity to experience all that we experience. We can readily see beauty and a sense of divinity everywhere we look.

Appreciation also opens our minds more widely to perceiving the subtle beauty all around us. It is through appreciation that beauty itself emerges. It is no coincidence that sages throughout time have shared a deep appreciation for the sublime elegance of what we call "reality."

Love

The next of the indices is **love**. The word "love" is one of the most confusing words in the English language. People use it to refer to a wide range of emotions and attitudes. One person from another culture once remarked, "Our language has seven different words to express the range of emotions that English speakers use the word 'love' for." It is not surprising that love is such a confusing subject in our culture. We've all heard statements like "I love you," "I love ice cream," and "God is love." Clearly, the meaning in each statement is very different. Even the statement "I love you" can mean very different things with different people and even with the same person in different contexts.

Love as one of the Indices of Consciousness is perhaps more clearly stated as "selfless love." It represents a free gift from the heart, without expectation of anything in return. In most instances, when people in romantic relationships say "I love you," the spoken words contain within them the unspoken message "and I expect your commitment." By "I love you," most people are not truly expressing "I value you because of who you are," but rather "I value you because you satisfy my needs." The collapse of these two contrary notions into the word "love" has created much confusion within our culture—hence the need to give careful consideration to the meaning behind the word's use. For purposes of this work, the needs-based version of "love" is not considered love.

Love, as one of the Indices of Consciousness, is the ability to see and value all people's needs and happiness as equally important to our own. When this trait is underdeveloped, we will exhibit a total lack of concern for anyone's welfare or needs other than our own. Whenever we give or make sacrifices for others, it is with the conscious or subconscious expectation that the favor will be returned. When this trait is functioning effectively, we will exhibit the same concern for others—within the constraints of our limits and responsibilities—as we do for ourselves. We will objectively weigh our needs and desires with others' needs and desires and will willingly make sacrifices to benefit the other person, regardless of whether the recipient ever can or will repay our goodness.

Emotional Discipline

The next of the indices is **emotional discipline**. Emotional discipline is the ability to delay or forgo gratification and to refrain from volatile emotions and mood swings. When this trait is under-developed, we will exhibit impulsive behavior and typically pursue immediate gratification. This can be in the form of satisfying a desire or avoiding discomfort. It is also difficult for us to follow rules, procedures, or reason if our emotions pull us in a different direction. When this trait is functioning effectively, we will exhibit control over our emotions and desires and readily forgo immediate gratification or endure present discomfort if a greater benefit can be obtained by doing so.

People in whom this trait is underdeveloped tend to experience wide or frequent swings in their emotions. Their experiences often affect them in deep, emotional ways. In extreme cases, underdeveloped emotional discipline can appear as manic or bipolar behavior.

Mental Discipline

The next of the indices is **mental discipline**. Mental discipline is the ability to control one's thoughts. When not preoccupied with external stimuli, the mind has a tendency to race and wander. Some have described the experience as an endless stream of thoughts, some surfacing in the conscious awareness and many flowing in the subconscious mind outside of awareness. When this trait is underdeveloped, we will allow random, counterproductive, and even destructive streams of thought to flow through our minds, and we are often unaware of many of them. When this trait is functioning effectively, we will be continuously aware of the thoughts that arise in our minds, and we will control our thinking. Destructive thoughts are discontinued, and the mental energies are rerouted to constructive thoughts. When this skill is well developed, we have the ability to stop our thoughts altogether and rest in complete mental silence.

An additional facet that is involved in mental discipline is being aware of and controlling the rapid chain of assumptions the mind will leap to in a fraction of a second. This is even more challenging for very bright people because their intelligence enables their minds to fly down chains of assumption, quickly carrying them beyond any reasonable relationship to their actual circumstances.

I once heard an attorney describing how, as a successful lawyer, he descended into deep depression and then alcoholism. He described one particular instance in which a client called to cancel an appointment with him. Because the client cancelled the appointment, the lawyer assumed the client must be unhappy. Because the client was unhappy, the attorney assumed the client would soon be firing him. Because the client was unhappy and going to fire him, the attorney assumed he must be doing something wrong, and he probably had other unhappy clients. Because he had several unhappy clients that were probably going to fire him, he assumed he would not have enough business to keep his law office open, and his income would cease. As a result of this, he would not be able to pay his mortgage and he would lose his house, becoming homeless.

This attorney was an intelligent man, but in a fraction of a second, his mind had created and accepted as true every assumption in his chain of thinking. Although he did not actually know why the client canceled the appointment, in the attorney's mind, this felt the same as being one step away from failing in business and becoming homeless. What he concluded this phone call meant was well beyond the facts he was presented with; his mind raced ahead, quickly leaving behind any reasonable relationship to the actuality of his circumstances. And so his thinking went with all of his daily events. Because he did not control this mental activity, he quickly arrived at unpleasant conclusions for most of his thoughts. As a result, almost everything that happened to him was devastating. I have seen this type of mind racing cause problems for many people, and, in general, the most pronounced cases have been in the most intelligent people.

Flexibility

The next of the indices is **flexibility**. Flexibility is the ability to accept, change, and adapt to new or unexpected circumstances. When this trait is underdeveloped, we will find it difficult to cope with or accept things that differ from our habits or expectations. When this trait is functioning effectively, we will be able to flow with whatever course circumstances may take, regardless of how much things may deviate from what we are habituated to or expecting. We are accepting of and make the most of whatever comes. We frequently exhibit and enjoy the benefits of innovative and creative approaches to circumstances and events and are open to recognizing and capitalizing on the opportunities they offer.

Positiveness

The next of the indices is **positiveness**. Positiveness is the ability to view the positive aspects of and possibilities within any situation, and to refrain from negative thoughts, words, and actions. When this trait is underdeveloped, we will approach things with the assumption that there is something bad or negative in any situation, and we will dwell on that aspect. We will constantly focus on how things could have been or should have been or ought to be better. If given a bowl of cherries, we will focus on and fret over the pits, frequently letting the cherries go to waste. When this trait is functioning effectively, we will seek out and find the positive aspects of things. We constantly focus on what is good and beneficial in things and events. We are skilled at finding and focusing on the silver lining in any cloud, and, if given a bowl of cherries, we will focus on and enjoy the cherries and either disregard the pits or find a constructive use for them.

Many people have had the experience of buying a new car and suddenly seeing that particular model everywhere. It becomes more pronounced in their awareness because of their focus on it. Positiveness works on the same principle. We can find good and bad in any situation, if we look for it. What we look for becomes more prominent in our world. Those who focus on the bad find their world filled with it. Those who focus on the good will likewise find their world filled with good. Moreover, a positive attitude toward the future will enable one to envision possibilities and opportunities that others will not see.

Positiveness is a valuable social skill. There's an old saying, "Laugh and the world laughs with you. Cry and you cry alone." People like being around others who are positive, much more so than they want to be around people who are constantly negative. As a result, positive people enjoy greater social opportunities and a wider circle of friends who enjoy their company.

Assertiveness

The next of the indices is **assertiveness**. Assertiveness is the ability to overcome silence, passivity, and inertia and to speak and act in accordance with who one truly is—without going to the opposite extreme of being domineering. When this trait is underdeveloped, while interacting with other people, we will either timidly withdraw, suppressing our true self and desires, or we go to the opposite extreme of forcing personal agendas on others. As a result, whether

it's ourselves or the others involved in the interaction, someone typically gets "run over." When this trait is functioning effectively, we
will be able, in a balanced way, to fully but tactfully express our
desires without putting others on the defensive or forcing our agenda
on them.

Objectivity

The next of the indices is **objectivity**. Objectivity is the ability
to see things from different perspectives and take a position against
oneself. When this trait is underdeveloped, we will only see things
as they appear from our own point of view. We are unable to "stand
outside ourselves" and assess things from a neutral perspective. In
our minds, we are always right. Typically, we will not accept or
respond well to any kind of criticism and will fail to see the help or
benefits offered from even benevolent and constructive criticism.
Because we believe ourselves to always be right, we will find it
extremely difficult, even when appropriate, to apologize. When this
trait is functioning effectively, we will be able to divorce our minds
from all of our history and assumptions and see things with "fresh
eyes." We will readily recognize and accept errors in our thinking or
behavior and have no difficulty apologizing when in the wrong.

A friend once described a process she used for overcoming
anger and frustration toward another friend. She said, "First, I
thought about how I felt about the situation. Then, I did my best
to really get inside the other person. I set aside all the judgments I
would normally make, and I imagined how she might feel toward
me and about the situation. I entertained the thought that I was not

perfect and perhaps had made some mistakes toward my friend. I also thought about all the things and stresses in her life that might be influencing her feelings. I tried to really let go of 'me' and really 'be' her for a while. It gave me a new perspective. Then I imagined myself as a third person who didn't know either one of us. I imagined how the third party might feel about the situation when viewing it from the outside. That enabled me to set aside the notion that either one of us was wrong, and recognize how an honest misunderstanding might have arisen. This empowered me to come back to 'myself' with a much broader, more objective view of the situation."

This process enabled my friend to step outside of her hurt and frustration and see the situation as someone else might. In doing so, her anger and frustration were left behind, and she was able to move forward with a sense of freedom she did not previously have. While the disagreement between her and her friend remained, she was able to stop seeing it as a personal attack and let go of the feeling of having been unfairly victimized. This skillful exercise of objectivity relieved my friend of a significant amount of emotional pain and turmoil.

In the high-stakes arena of the legal field, objectivity is a critical mental skill. Attorneys are trained to understand the opponent's side of the case just as well as their own. They objectively evaluate every weakness, flaw, and mistake in their own case. In doing so, they are able to come to a much better understanding of the case and to see it how a judge or jury might view it. Those who fail in this skill are quickly shown to be woefully lacking in insight. Applying this same skill to everyday situations can significantly improve one's ability to make wise decisions.

Communication

The next of the indices is **communication**. Communication is the ability to convey to others accurate pictures of what we are thinking or feeling and to obtain accurate understandings from others of what they are thinking or feeling. When this trait is underdeveloped, we will have difficulty either listening to or actually understanding what another person is trying to express. We may also experience difficulty in successfully conveying our own thoughts or feelings. When this trait is functioning effectively, we will be adept at sending and receiving accurate information. This is not to say that miscommunication never occurs, but it happens much less frequently, and when it does, we are skilled at recognizing and correcting the miscommunication that has taken place.

In a sense, communication is a composite ability. It is built upon many other important skills such as empathy, intuition, objectivity, and good listening. All of these contribute to our ability to communicate effectively, as does our command of grammar and vocabulary.

Awareness

The final of the indices is **awareness**. Awareness is our ability to consciously recognize the emotions and thoughts we experience, as we experience them. When this trait is underdeveloped, we will frequently be driven by our subconscious, experiencing thoughts and feelings with no idea of what led to them. Being unaware of what brought these into being, we lack the ability to modify our thinking and reactions. As a result, we remain trapped in negative ruts that cause us unhappiness and pain. When this trait is functioning effectively, we will be cognizant of our thoughts and feelings as they arise. Consequently, we are able to recognize and follow the chain of reactions that flow from the cause. As a result, we develop a recognition of the origin of our pain and unhappiness and are able to dismantle harmful patterns of thought, freeing ourselves from the pain and from counterproductive habits of thought and reaction.

Questions for Group or Individual Exploration

A list of the Twenty-One Indices is included below for easy reference. Appendix B features quotes from some of history's highest achievers about the topics represented within the Twenty-One Indices. The people quoted represent a wide and diverse range of cultures and times in history.

1. Honesty

2. Egalitarianism

3. Equanimity

4. Faith

5. Responsibility

6. Balance

7. Empathy

8. Nonjudgmentalism

9. Open-mindedness

10. Presentness

11. Courage

12. Appreciation

13. Love

14. Emotional Discipline

15. Mental Discipline

16. Flexibility

17. Positiveness

18. Assertiveness

19. Objectivity

20. Communication

21. Awareness

1. What are some examples from literature or history where you have heard some of the Indices of Consciousness put forward as pearls of wisdom?

2. What are some examples you have observed where being underdeveloped in one of the Indices has decreased a person's happiness?

3. Think of the adult person you know who functions most effectively in the most Indices of Consciousness. How do you think this person would describe his or her life?

4. Think of the adult person you know who functions least effectively in the most Indices of Consciousness. How do you think this person would describe his or her life?

5. When you compare the previous two people, what thoughts does this raise in your mind?

Benjamin Franklin's Thirteen Virtues

The Twenty-One Indices of Consciousness provide a useful checklist for analytical reference. But even the best conceptual construct is useless without practical application. It is one thing to recognize their usefulness; it is another thing to integrate them into our being. Fortunately, Ben Franklin, one of America's leading philosophers, inventors, and statesmen, had some very practical advice to offer. As a young man, Franklin formulated a list of thirteen virtues he felt were key to establishing an honorable and productive character in a person. He recognized the difficulty of trying to assimilate all of them effectively into his mind and daily practice, so Franklin devised a plan for developing his chosen virtues. He would study his list each day to evaluate his progress on each, but he would intentionally focus on one virtue above all others each week. Then he would move to the next virtue the following week. In this way, he found himself able to progress in one virtue while holding his ground in the others. By the end of the year, he had circulated through his list four times. He considered this intentional and systematic formation of his character the bedrock of his wisdom and success. He went on to be widely respected by his countrymen even to this day. The following are excerpts from Franklin's autobiography, detailing his process:

> It was about this time I conceived the bold and arduous project of arriving at moral perfection. I wished to live without committing any fault at any time; I would conquer all that either natural inclination, custom, or company might lead me into. As I knew, or thought I knew, what was right and wrong, I did not see why I might not always do the one and avoid the other. But I soon found I had undertaken a task of more difficulty than I had imagined. While my care was employed in guarding against one fault, I was often surprised by another; habit took the advantage of inattention; inclination was sometimes too strong for reason. I concluded, at length, that the mere speculative conviction that it was our interest to be completely virtuous was not sufficient to prevent our slipping; and that the contrary habits must be broken, and good ones acquired and established, before we can have any dependence on a steady, uniform rectitude of conduct. For this purpose I therefore contrived the following method . . .
>
> My intention being to acquire the habitude of all these virtues, I judged it would be well not to distract my attention by attempting the whole at once, but to fix it on one of them at a time; and, when I should be master of that, then

to proceed to another, and so on, till I should have gone through the thirteen . . . Conceiving then, that, agreeably to the advice of Pythagoras in his Golden Verses, daily examination would be necessary, I contrived the following method for conducting that examination.

I made a little book, in which I allotted a page for each of the virtues. I ruled each page with red ink, so as to have seven columns, one for each day of the week, marking each column with a letter for the day. I crossed these columns with thirteen red lines, marking the beginning of each line with the first letter of one of the virtues, on which line, and in its proper column, I might mark, by a little black spot, every fault I found upon examination to have been committed respecting that virtue upon that day.

I determined to give a week's strict attention to each of the virtues successively. Thus, in the first week, my great guard was to avoid every the least offence against Temperance, leaving the other virtues to their ordinary chance, only marking every evening the faults of the day. Thus, if in the first week I could keep my first line, marked T, clear of spots, I supposed the habit of that virtue so much strengthened and its opposite weakened, that I might venture extending my attention to include the next, and for the following week keep both lines clear of spots. Proceeding thus to the last, I could go through a course complete in thirteen weeks, and four courses in a year. And like him who, having a garden to weed, does not attempt to eradicate all the bad herbs at once, which would exceed his reach and his strength, but works on one of the beds at a time, and, having accomplished the first, proceeds to a second, so I should have, I hoped, the encouraging pleasure of seeing on my pages the progress I made in virtue, by clearing successively my lines of their spots, till in the end, by a number of courses, I should be happy in viewing a clean book, after a thirteen weeks' daily examination.[42]

Franklin's method offers a tried and true approach to cultivating a chosen set of mental habits, the aim of the Twenty-One Indices of Consciousness. A similar chart for the Twenty-One Indices of Consciousness is freely downloadable at www.AppliedConsciousnessSystems. com. This chart is a useful tool for individual consciousness work and for organizing group discussions. For example, a study group might use the chart as a regular discussion guide, picking one of the indices to discuss at their next meeting, and observing its operation in their lives between meetings. When the group meets, members are likely to have a wide range of examples of how that particular index has affected them. By discussing their diverse experiences, the group can have a broader exploration of each one of the Indices of Consciousness, and how it affects people's lives.

Questions for Group or Individual Exploration

1. What general similarities do you see between virtues and Indices of Consciousness?

2. What general differences do you see between virtues and Indices of Consciousness?

3. Based on your observation of people, do you think Franklin's belief in the importance of a daily review of one's goals is important? Why or why not?

4. Based on your life experiences and your observations of people, do you think Franklin's organized, methodical approach to self-improvement is a good one? Why or why not?

5. How might Franklin's investment in his inner qualities have contributed to his outward success?

6. How easy or difficult have you found it to make and/or break habits? Why do you believe this is so?

7. How might Franklin's method be compared to the process of learning to drive a car?

I Am the Wave

In summary, when we look beyond the language and the cultures from which they spoke and consider the essence of their messages, the cumulative and consistent advice of our greatest minds can be summarized as follows: "The greatest investment you could ever make is in your consciousness. You deserve it, and the world needs it." Evolving our consciousness is the surest way forward for humanity. When we look at consciousness as the common living fabric across humanity, it appears as a great unbroken ocean. The actions we take and the thoughts we think are ripples in that ocean. Through it, those ripples touch and affect everything that is. While this work has focused on theory, theory is useless without application. As has been previously alluded to, the coming evolutionary leap forward for humanity will not be made by a handful of inspired leaders. It will be brought about by the collective efforts of millions and millions of ordinary people. The participation and responsibility falls to each of us as individuals to do our part in moving humanity forward. Once this realization began to sink in for me, I came to this realization: I *am* the wave. Each of us is. As millions and millions of tiny ripples join in synergistic harmony, a tidal wave of consciousness will rise. As we become the paradigm and make it real within how we think and act, we come to live in the reality that *we* are the wave.

In my life's journey, I find, interestingly enough, that I have come full circle to my point of origin. My life's quest has returned to where it began many years ago. In ways, I am still the kid trying to understand the world around me and how I can best contribute to its betterment and improve the lives of my fellow humans. But my thinking and models for contemplation have evolved and grown much more complex. Instead of people and objects, I view things in terms of consciousness and energy. I've been the beneficiary of some of our greatest minds' thoughts on the nature of reality, life, and happiness. I continue to feel an overwhelming sense of mission and responsibility for improving the welfare of our world. I feel even more acutely now that I came here with the purpose of serving others—but how I see others has changed. Through consciousness, I see connections I did not see as a youth. My life's journey and new perspectives have raised pivotal questions within me. Can changing our consciousness significantly change our experience of life? Can raising our consciousness really make us a lot happier and make the world a better place? Is investing in raising consciousness really worth the effort? For me, the answer to all these questions is "Yes!"

Having had the interest and the motivation to read this book, you are already an integral and invaluable contributor to raising human consciousness. The thrust of this work has been to review some of the benefits of raising consciousness and to propose a paradigm for how we can best move forward. One of its aims is to instigate a broad social discussion of the issues. Talk to people about consciousness. Share your thoughts and consider theirs. Whether you support or oppose the proposed paradigm as the best approach, your active participation in the discussion will help focus attention on the matter. This, in and of itself, will serve to raise humanity's consciousness. The more perspectives we can raise, include, and harmonize within the debate, the more cohesive, illumined, and powerful our collective consciousness will become.

While the consciousness paradigm is structured around and discussed in terms of its application to individuals, its principles apply to broader society as well. Lower levels of consciousness can typically be seen as the drivers behind wars, religious fanaticism, genocide, the decimation of natural resources, and many other globally significant trends. By elevating the global Level of Consciousness, society can be better equipped to more successfully and less destructively meet the challenges we face now and in the future.

Consider a country led by a consciousness centered at the instinctual level. It is not difficult to imagine how differently it would interact with the world when compared to a country led by a consciousness centered at the rational level. At the macro level, the instinctually led country would behave comparably to an individual who is functioning at the same level. But as a nation, its destructive capacity would be vastly greater than any individual's.

Imagine a world in which consciousness skills are taught as a regular part of public education around the globe. It does not take much to envision how different our world would be if a pluralistic consciousness was the norm. As democracy spreads around the globe, the Level of Consciousness of our elected officials becomes a more important criterion for voter consideration. In the free world, it is, after all, we the people who choose the leaders. As the power and numbers of "we the people" grows ever greater, we are the ones who will (or at least should) determine the course of the future.

Paradise is not a place, but a state of consciousness, and raising global consciousness is our best hope for Earth's future. While the consciousness paradigm is a totally new concept in most people's minds, the capacity for its rapid spread around the globe is a reality. The future will not be transformed into the greatest of our visions without harnessing the collective will. The paradigm of consciousness offers a common language and an easily accessible scaffolding for organizing individual thought and public discussion around the mechanics of maximizing our experience of, and contribution to, life.

The emerging consciousness movement is literally changing the way we view ourselves, our lives, and the world we live in. The more we can share, contribute to, and engage in the discussion, the faster we can reap the benefits. A tidal shift in consciousness will not arise by the heroic efforts of a few highly enlightened individuals; they have already done their part. This transformation and evolution of humanity will sweep the globe one person, one e-mail, and one conversation at a time. The signs are everywhere that it is already under way. The last and final word of this work is not a statement, but a request. If you haven't already done so, please join in this revolution! Be the wave. Raising your consciousness is one of the greatest gifts you can give yourself and the world. But don't accept the consciousness paradigm or its assertions without critical analysis. Put them to the test. See if they prove true in your experience. Apply them in your mind *and* in your actions, and let the results be the measure of their worth. But do try them . . . because the path to a brighter future runs through you!

Questions for Group or Individual Exploration

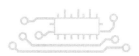

1. Within your life experiences, what are some of the ways people might benefit the most from raising consciousness?

2. What methods can you think of that would be helpful for applying the Twenty-One Indices of Consciousness in people's lives?

3. What are some ways you or your group might contribute to the public discussion of consciousness?

4. What are some ways you or your group might contribute to raising consciousness?

5. What would you like the world to be like in 100 years?

6. What do you think are some of the best means we have for getting there?

Appendix A

The Sunrise Meditation Method

One definition of consciousness is the ability of a system to respond to stimuli. Consciousness can also be thought of as awareness. Thus, as it relates to the Sunrise Meditation Method, a method I developed, consciousness can be thought of as a person's awareness of and ability to respond to stimuli. Within the Sunrise Meditation Method, the starting process for raising or expanding one's consciousness is to increase his or her alertness to what is happening in any given moment. In the early stages, this means becoming more mindful of the thoughts and feelings going on inside oneself. As consciousness is raised, the additional layer of increased awareness of one's environment is added.

The Two-Part Process to Elevating Consciousness

In organizing the initial approach to meditating, it is helpful to think of it in two parts:

1. Continuously observing what you are feeling.

2. Continuously observing what you are thinking.

The Sunrise Meditation Method begins by paying close attention to what happens within you. Every minute of every day, you should be keenly aware of the feelings and emotions that are going on in your body and the thoughts that are going through your head. For the vast majority of people, most of these things run in the background, and they are only aware of the product of these processes.

Part One: Sharpen Awareness of Stimuli That Influence Feelings

Many people are aware of feelings they have, but are not aware of exactly how those feelings arose. For example, a person may realize that he is angry. However, that anger may only be the end result of a complex internal process. The anger may be only a portion of what he is feeling. And while there may be many other feelings below the surface, the anger is the only one that grew strong enough to actually surface in his conscious awareness. Without stopping and thinking about it, the person may not know exactly what made him angry. He may be aware that he was angered by a conversation he just had, but he doesn't know which specific words rubbed him the wrong way or why. Nor does he know what feelings were initially triggered that led to his anger. Perhaps it was just one sentence that made him feel insulted, that bruised his pride. Perhaps it was one small comment that triggered one of his insecurities. Perhaps something came across as a threat, which caused fear. Many times a small thing causes a person to "blow up" because it is the proverbial straw that broke the camel's back. Most people are unaware of all the straw the camel is carrying before the final straw comes crashing down. Effective meditation will bring these issues into a person's conscious awareness so they can be dealt with, and the camel can be "unburdened."

Those who are consciously aware of their feelings will recognize the instant someone says something that upsets them. They will be aware of exactly which words irritated them and why. They will also be aware of what feelings and thoughts arise within them as a result. Because of this, they can observe the chain of reactions that follow. This kind of awareness is called source awareness. These people are aware of the source (or trigger) of the flow of thoughts or emotions that they experience. Once you achieve source awareness, you gain control over your reactions. You can control or break the chain of emotional and mental reactions that would otherwise occur automatically, outside your awareness.

Source awareness provides control and opens the door to our greater mind. In addition to gaining control over their reactions, people who have source awareness gain familiarity with how external events affect their thoughts and feelings. Once they have achieved this, when they encounter energy or feelings that have no apparent external cause, they know to look deeper within themselves. The feelings could be arising out of their subconscious, or they could be messages coming from the greater mind. Having this awareness and understanding enables you to recognize the messages and guidance your greater mind sends you, always with the aim of helping you experience the richest and most fulfilling life possible.

Part Two: Sharpen Awareness of Assumptions, Beliefs, and the Flow of Thought

The second part of raising/expanding consciousness is expanding our frame of reference. This process is primarily mental and has to do with the way we think and the assumptions and beliefs we hold. It involves continually expanding the points of view that we take into account when making decisions. The more information we have, the better the decision we can make. Likewise, the more points of view we are capable of drawing from in evaluating a situation, the better the understanding we will have.

Elevating the mental aspect of consciousness is a process of continually expanding the frame of reference within which we operate. One example comes from the school-age years. Most people are familiar with the intense pain experienced by some "crisis" they experienced during their years in school. At the time, the crisis seemed monumental. But when later viewed in the context of the person's entire life, it was really a trivial occurrence. The same is true when considering present life events. When viewed from the perspective of this one life, they may seem major or even devastating. But when our greater minds view things from the perspective of many lives, the significance of these events shrinks dramatically. Likewise, viewing life from the perspective of the greater mind drastically reduces fear and anxiety. The "worst" that can happen in this life (death) is of little significance to the greater mind.

The Four Practices of the Sunrise Method

The following Sunrise Method practices may be helpful in forming habits that will cultivate your awareness and elevate your consciousness.

1. Make Time for Solitude

The best way to begin raising your consciousness is to observe solitude time. In order to do this, it is vitally important to set aside at least fifteen minutes each day. This time should be considered and treated as sacred time that you devote to yourself. Find a quiet place, and arrange your schedule so you will have no interruptions. Some people find it helpful to burn a candle or incense to set the mood. Some like to play soothing music in the background. If you choose to play background music, it should be soft, relaxing, and instrumental. However, if you find the music distracting, complete silence would likely be a better approach for you.

Another aid to effective solitude time is selecting the right place. Ideally, you should find a corner of your home, or at least a chair, that you will *only* use during your solitude time. Specifically limiting the space or chair that you use helps train your mind. You take advantage of the habitual and frequently subconscious associations your mind attaches to the things you interact with regularly. You become accustomed to focusing quickly on your inner processes.

Place yourself in a comfortable, seated position. Relax completely and close your eyes. Closing your eyes helps you focus internally, within yourself. Be consciously aware of all the thoughts and feelings you experience during this time. The more continuously and clearly you can be aware of what is going on within you, the better. Building this internal awareness will prepare you for the other exercises.

2. Clear the Hamper

During solitude time, you will become more aware of the thoughts and feelings you are experiencing within yourself. As you sit quietly, thoughts will arise that often don't surface during the active times of the day, when your attention is focused on other things. Frequently, things occur that trigger certain reactions that we don't have time to deal with right then, so the mind stuffs them into what could be called the mental laundry hamper for later processing. This enables the mind to focus on what is, at that moment, an issue of higher priority. The feelings and thoughts that get stuffed in the hamper sit there until they are processed or forgotten. However, some things exhibit a tenacious resistance to being completely forgotten, even though they may hide below the surface for long periods of time.

During solitude time, we have a quiet, uninterrupted space in which we can focus on subtler things. When we relax and open our minds in solitude, things in the hamper tend to "bubble" up to the surface of our consciousness, where we can think about and process them. To help us remember important issues, our subconscious minds have a tendency to fixate on those issues until we have dealt with them. Once the demands on our attention diminish and the opportunity arises, our subconscious will remind us of these "back burner" items.

Keeping a notepad handy during solitude time is useful. On it, we can write down the back burner issues that arise out of our mental hampers. As our skill at using solitude time increases, we are able to dig deeper and deeper into the mental hamper. In doing so, many issues will surface. Some will be deep, personal issues that affect how we view and experience life. We will also uncover issues that are mundane or less important. While these mundane issues may be important or even urgent, they don't really relate to understanding who we are. For example, during solitude time, we may remember that we need to purchase a get well card for a friend who is ill. While this may be important, it is not the type of issue we want to focus on during solitude. But because it is important, our subconscious will tend to keep bringing it up until we get it done. However, if we write down a note to ourselves on our notepad, we consciously acknowledge and memorialize the concern. Knowing that this issue has been physically preserved for later processing allows our subconscious to let go of it and move on to other, more subtle issues.

If we regularly "dig into our hamper" and process what is in there, over time, we will travel deeper and deeper within ourselves. Separating out the mundane issues and writing them on the notepad frees us to concentrate on those issues that will actually change our lives.

3. Quiet the Mind

During your solitude time, clear your mind of all distractions. Empty it of any thoughts of responsibilities at work and home and other chores you need to do. Write these on your notepad as, one by one, you empty your hamper. Focus completely on quieting your mind so you are able to maintain a quiet, relaxed state of inner silence.

When first attempted, quieting the mind is difficult for most people. Without conscious attention, the mind tends to produce a constant flow of mental "chatter." Learning to quiet this chatter is an invaluable skill. If you feel your mind wandering, just gently redirect it toward quiet stillness. As your skill improves, you gain a greater ability to filter out distractions. It is like turning down the volume on a loud radio so you can hear the quieter, more subtle sounds. Once you have the ability to quiet your mind, you can easily focus your attention on exactly what you want to. You are also able to hear the deeper, subtler messages your subconscious mind and your greater mind send you.

4. Write in a Journal

Journaling is similar to the process of clearing the hamper. Except that instead of writing down the mundane things, you write down the important things. Journaling focuses on the issues that lead to a better understanding of yourself. It serves as a log of important ideas and trains of thought. As you wrestle with things about yourself that you want to better understand, change, or control, your journal is your record of where you have been.

Journaling serves two important functions. First, it helps break circular thought patterns. It is the nature of the mind to continually work on unresolved problems until they are solved or go away. What often results is somewhat obsessive or compulsive thinking, repeating the same thoughts over and over. Journaling entails thinking through an issue as thoroughly as possible and then writing down all of your significant thoughts on the subject. Then, make and keep a commitment to yourself that you will not think about the subject again until you schedule a time, journal in hand, to consider it again. If you find yourself randomly thinking about the subject during the day, make yourself stop until you intentionally decide to spend time thinking about it once again. At first it takes a little practice, but once the subconscious is trained in how you want it to handle such thoughts, this approach becomes much easier. Once we get used to this, our mind is able to let go of journaled subjects, at least until the facts of the situation change.

Again, formally memorializating the subject matter and every possible approach to the situation that we can think of frees our mind to focus on other things. Going back to the subject and rehashing the thinking we already worked through and committed to paper feels like beating a dead horse. As a result, our mental energy is directed to new approaches and new ways of looking at things rather than just rehashing the same old stuff. We go from circular thinking to forward-moving thinking.

The second important function of journaling is to record the course of our progress. Many times, journal entries contain wisdom and insights that don't surface until later readings. What may seem like an insignificant side comment when written can turn out to be the exact key to solving a situation that arises weeks or months later. Additionally, it records the evolution in our thinking and spiritual growth. Many people don't realize how far they've come until they go back and read their journal entries from the previous year. Oftentimes they are surprised at how "primitive" their old approaches seem.

Finally, as one compiles a journal over time, the journal becomes a map of sorts. This map provides markers showing where we have been and the route we have taken to get to where we are. Seeing this trail often serves as a pointer, giving us a powerful hint of where we are headed in the future.

Because a journal is intended to hold the most personal and significant thoughts and feelings of an individual, it should be treated with respect. Invest in a nice writing journal that symbolizes the importance of the information it will contain. Ideally, the type and style of the journal should have personal meaning to you.

Appendix B

Quotes Addressing the Twenty-One Indices of Consciousness

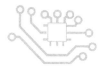

$\mathfrak{M}$any of history's wisest have pondered and commented upon the topics that make up the Twenty-One Indices. A sampling has been compiled for each one of the indices, for purposes of reflection, and to illustrate the diversity of people who have espoused each principle. Though not as familiar as the Golden Rule, these precepts have a similarly broad list of proponents, of which those cited represent only a small portion.

○

1. *Honesty*—a commitment to accurate, straightforward, and unbiased thoughts, words, and self-assessment, despite the discomfort it may cause.

> This above all: to thine own self be true, and it must follow, as the night the day. Thou canst not then be false to any man.
>
> —Shakespeare

I hope I shall always possess firmness and virtue enough
to maintain what I consider the most enviable of all titles,
the character of an honest man.

—George Washington

Nothing is easier than self-deceit. For what each man
wishes, that he also believes to be true.

—Demosthenes

Let us be true: this is the highest maxim of art and of life,
the secret of eloquence and of virtue, and of all moral
authority.

—Henri Amiel

Truthful lips will be established forever, but a lying tongue
is only for a moment.

—Proverbs 12:19

A lying tongue hates those it crushes, and a flattering
mouth works ruin.

—Proverbs 26:28

A truthful witness saves lives, but he who speaks lies is
treacherous.

—Proverbs 14:25

2. *Egalitarianism*—a view that all humans are equal in worth, regardless of their respective talents, successes, failures, flaws, status, or assets.

> Wherever there is a human being, I see God-given
> rights inherent in that being, whatever may be the sex
> or complexion.
>
> —William Lloyd Garrison

> Unless a man is committed to the belief that all of
> mankind are his brothers, then he labors in vain and
> hypocritically in the vineyards of equality.
>
> —Adam Clayton Powell

> This nation was founded by men of many nations and
> backgrounds. It was founded on the principle that all men
> are created equal, and that the rights of every man are
> diminished when the rights of one man are threatened.
>
> —John F. Kennedy

> He who shuts his ear to the cry of the poor will also cry
> himself and not be answered.
>
> —Proverbs 21:13

> We hold these truths to be self-evident, that all men are
> created equal, that they are endowed by their creator
> with certain unalienable rights, that among those are life,
> liberty, and the pursuit of happiness.
>
> —Thomas Jefferson/Declaration of Independence

All, too, will bear in mind this sacred principle, that
though the will of the majority is in all cases to prevail,
that will to be rightful must be reasonable; that the
minority possess their equal rights, which equal law must
protect, and to violate would be oppression.

—Thomas Jefferson

Pride goes before destruction, and a haughty spirit before
stumbling.

—Proverbs 16:18

○

3. *Equanimity*—**equal-minded acceptance of things and circumstances outside the person's reasonable sphere of control, and
acceptance of intrinsic value in all things, regardless of one's
personal preferences.**

He who is of equal mind in pain and pleasure, centered
in himself, to whom a lump of earth, a stone, or gold
are as one; who is of equal mind with those who love
or dislike him, constant, the same whether blamed or
praised; equally minded in honor and disgrace, and the
same toward friendly or unfriendly side, engaging only in
necessary actions, he has truly excelled.

—Bhagavad-Gita

He who has endured such vicissitudes with equanimity
has deprived misfortune of its power.

—Seneca

The less justified a man is in claiming excellence for his own self, the more ready is he to claim all excellence for his nation, his religion, his race or his holy cause.

—Eric Hoffer

Political extremism involves two prime ingredients: an excessively simple diagnosis of the world's ills and a conviction that there are identifiable villains back of it all.

—John W. Gardner

○

4. *Faith*—belief that good exists and can be found in, or created from, any circumstance.

If you resist your fate, it will trample you and drag you along behind it, but if you embrace your fate, it will guide you.

—Seneca

Faith is to believe what you do not see; the reward for faith is to see what you believe.

—St. Augustine

A man consists of the faith that is in him. Whatever his faith is, he is.

—Bhagavad-Gita

The care of God for us is a great thing, if a man believe it at heart; it plucks the burden of sorrow from him.

—Euripides

Hope looks for unqualified success; but faith counts certainly on failure and takes honorable defeat to be a form of victory.

—Robert Louis Stevenson

○

5. *Responsibility*—**willingness to be held accountable for one's actions and willingness to take on and successfully execute to the best of one's ability, tasks that rightly fall to him or her.**

I am inclined to believe that a man may be free to do anything he pleases if only he will accept responsibility for whatever he does.

—Ellen Glasgow

To be a man is, precisely, to be responsible.

—Saint-Exupery

God obligeth no man to more than he hath given him ability to perform.

—Koran

When duty comes a-knocking at your gate, welcome him in; for if you bid him wait, he will depart only to come once more and bring seven other duties to your door.

—Edwin Markham

He that is good for making excuses is seldom good for anything else.

—Benjamin Franklin

6. *Balance*—**the ability to constructively manage and integrate competing demands, desires, or perspectives.**

> Nothing in excess.
>
> —Solon

> There is nobody as enslaved as the fanatic, the person in whom one impulse, one value, has assumed ascendancy over all others.
>
> —Milton Sapirstein

> It is only through restraint that man can manage not to suppress himself.
>
> —Andre Gide

> In everything the middle course is best; all things in excess bring trouble.
>
> —Plautus

> Moderation is the silken string running through the pearl chain of all virtues.
>
> —Joseph Hall

> It is well to moor your boat with two anchors.
>
> —Publilius Syrus

○

7. *Empathy*—the ability to accurately perceive another person's perspective and emotional state.

> Until we know what motivates the hearts and minds of men we can understand nothing outside ourselves, nor will we ever reach fulfillment as that greatest miracle of all, the human being.
>
> —Marya Mannes

> A man, to be greatly good, must imagine intensely and comprehensively; he must put himself in the place of another and of many others; the pains and pleasures of his species must become his own.
>
> —Percey Bysshe Shelley

> Each of us really understands in others only those feelings he is capable of producing himself.
>
> —Andre Gide

○

8. *Nonjudgmentalism*—the practice of refraining from making assumptions about other people's motives, or engaging in critical or demeaning lines of thought toward another's value as a person.

> Judge not, lest ye be judged.
>
> —Jesus

Don't judge a man until you've walked a mile in his moccasins.

—American Indian proverb

When we come to judge others it is not by ourselves as we really are that we judge them, but by an image that we have formed of ourselves from which we have left out everything that offends our vanity or would discredit us in the eyes of the world.

—W. Somerset Maugham

Such as every man is inwardly so he judgeth outwardly.

—Thomas à Kempis

Self-righteousness is a loud din raised to drown the voice of guilt within us.

—Eric Hoffer

Men never do evil so completely and cheerfully as when they do it from a religious conviction.

—Pascal

As in water face reflects face, so the heart of man reflects man.

—Proverbs 27:19

What you meet in another being is the projection of your own level of evolution.

—Ram Dass

○

9. *Open-mindedness*—**the ability to comfortably receive and objectively reflect on ideas, practices, or experiences that are outside one's habituated norm.**

> The beautiful souls are they that are universal, open, and ready for all things.
>
> —Montaigne

> If there is anything more dangerous to the life of the mind than having no independent commitment to ideas, it is having an excess of commitment to some special idea.
>
> —Richard Hofstadter

> The way of a fool is right in his own eyes, but a wise man is he who listens to counsel.
>
> —Proverbs 12:15

> Sincerity that thinks it is the sole possessor of the truth is a deadlier sin than hypocrisy, which knows better.
>
> —Sydney J. Harris

> I am not so much concerned with the right of everyone to say anything he pleases as I am about our need as a self-governing people to hear everything relevant.
>
> —John F. Kennedy

> The most fatal illusion is the settled point of view. Since life is growth and motion, a fixed point of view kills anybody who has one.
>
> —Brooks Atkinson

Beware of the man of one book.

—St. Thomas Aquinas

Do not reprove a scoffer, lest he hate you. Reprove a wise man, and he will love you. Give instruction to a wise man and he will be still wiser. Teach a righteous man and he will increase his learning.

—Proverbs 9:8–9

○

10. *Presentness*—**the ability to maintain full conscious awareness upon the here and now.**

Real generosity toward the future lies in giving all to the present.

—Albert Camus

Remember that the sole life which a man can lose is that which he is living at the moment.

—Marcus Aurelius

We can easily manage if we will only take, each day, the burden appointed to it. But the load will be too heavy for us if we carry yesterday's burden over again today, and then add the burden of the morrow before we are required to bear it.

—John Newton

The living moment is everything.

—D.H. Lawrence

Rejoice in the things that are present; all else is
beyond thee.

—Montaigne

Yesterday is history. Tomorrow is a mystery. And today?
Today is a gift. That's why we call it the present.
—Babatunde Olatunji

We crucify ourselves between two thieves: regret for
yesterday and fear of tomorrow.
—Fulton Oursler

The ability to be in the present moment is a major component of mental wellness.
—Abraham Maslow

Be here now.

—Ram Dass

One of the most tragic things I know about human nature
is that all of us tend to put off living. We are all dreaming
of some magical rose garden over the horizon—instead of
enjoying the roses that are blooming outside our windows
today.
—Dale Carnegie

○

11. *Courage*—the inner strength and resolve to face and deal with things that are uncomfortable but necessary.

> All of the significant battles are waged within the self.
> —Sheldon Kopp

> Braver is the man who faces his own shortcomings and demons, than he who faces an army.
> —Anonymous

> Life without the courage for death is slavery.
> —Seneca

> Courage is a kind of salvation.
> —Plato

> Courage is the thing. All goes if courage goes.
> —J.M. Barrie

> Unless we can bear self-mortification, we shall not be able to carry self-examination to the necessary painful lengths. Without humility, there can be no illuminating self-knowledge.
> —Arnold Toynbee

> There's a lot of fear connected with the inner journey because it penetrates our illusions. Taking the inner journey will lead you into some very shadowy places. You're going to learn things about yourself that you'll wish you didn't know. There are monsters in there—monsters you

can't control—but trying to keep them hidden will only give them greater power.

—Parker Palmer

Valor lies just halfway between rashness and cowheartedness.

—Cervantes

The paradox of courage is that a man must be a little careless of his life even in order to keep it.

—G.K. Chesterton

That man is not truly brave who is afraid either to seem to be, or to be, when it suits him, a coward.

—Edgar Allen Poe

○

12. *Appreciation*—the ability to find and appreciate qualities of goodness and beauty in all things.

He who can no longer pause to wonder and stand rapt in awe is as good as dead; his eyes are closed.

—Albert Einstein

Let's trade in all our judging for appreciating. Let's lay down our righteousness and just be together.

—Ram Dass

If the only prayer you said in your whole life was "thank you," that would suffice.

—Meister Eckhart

I would maintain that thanks are the highest form of thought, and that gratitude is happiness doubled by wonder.

—Gilbert K. Chesterton

We can only be said to be alive in those moments when our hearts are conscious of our treasures.

—Thornton Wilder

One must ask children and birds how cherries and strawberries taste.

—Goethe

To speak truly, few adult persons can see nature. Most persons do not see the sun. At least they have a very superficial seeing. The sun illuminates only the eye of the man, but shines into the eye and heart of the child. The lover of nature is he whose inward and outward senses are still truly adjusted to each other; who has retained the spirit of infancy even into the era of manhood.

—Ralph Waldo Emerson

A child's world is fresh and new and beautiful, full of wonder and excitement. It is our misfortune that for most of us that clear-eyed vision, that true instinct for what is beautiful and awe-inspiring is dimmed and even lost before we reach adulthood.

—Rachel Carson

○

13. *Love*—**the ability and practice of valuing others' happiness as equally important to one's own.**

> Love is patient, love is kind; it is not jealous; love does not brag and is not arrogant, does not act unbecomingly; it does not seek its own, is not provoked, does not take into account a wrong suffered, does not rejoice in unrighteousness, but rejoices with the truth, bears all things, believes all things, hopes all things, endures all things, love never fails.
>
> —I Corinthians 13, 4 8

> Love does not cause suffering: what causes it is the sense of ownership, which is love's opposite.
>
> —Saint-Exupery

> Him that I love, I wish to be free—even from me.
>
> —Anne Morrow Lindbergh

> There is no fear in love; but perfect love casteth out fear.
>
> —I John 4:13

> Love is all we have, the only way that each can help the other.
>
> —Euripides

> When the power of love overcomes the love of power, then the world will know peace.
>
> —Jimi Hendrix

Love is the true price of love.

—George Herbert

The supreme happiness of life is the conviction that we are loved.

—Victor Hugo

We cannot love ourselves unless we love others, and we cannot love others unless we love ourselves. But a selfish love of ourselves makes us incapable of loving others.

—Thomas Merton

Love knows hidden paths.

—German proverb

○

14. *Emotional Discipline*—the ability to restrain the emotions and to avoid thinking or behaving impulsively or irrationally.

The human heart is like a ship on a stormy sea driven about by winds blowing from all four corners of heaven.

—Martin Luther

When the passions become masters, they are vices.

—Pascal

Serving one's own passions is the greatest slavery.

—Thomas Fuller

Freedom is not procured by a full enjoyment of what is
desired, but by controlling the desire.

—Epictetus

He that would be superior to external influences must first
become superior to his own passions.

—Samuel Johnson

One ought to hold on to one's heart; for if one lets it go,
one soon loses control of the head, too.

—Nietzsche

The heart has such an influence over the understanding
that it is worthwhile to engage it in our interest.

—Lord Chesterfield

The way to avoid evil is not by maiming our passions, but
by compelling them to yield their vigor to our
moral nature.

—Henry Ward Beecher

All emotions are pure which gather you and lift you up;
that emotion is impure which seizes only one side of your
being and so distorts you.

—Rainer Maria Rilke

A woman holds dreadful power over a man who is in love
with her, but she should realize that the quality and force
of his love is the index of his potential contempt
and hatred.

—John Steinbeck

He who is slow to anger has great understanding. But he
who is quick tempered exalts folly. A tranquil heart is life
to the body. But passion is rottenness to the bones.

—Proverbs 14:29 30

Take heed lest passion sway thy judgment to do aught,
which else free will would not admit.

—Milton

○

**15. *Mental Discipline*—the ability to maintain order in one's
thoughts and constrain the mind from wandering, indulging in
illogical assumptions, or pursuing destructive or negative lines
of thinking.**

Pushing any truth out very far, you are met by
a counter-truth.

—Henry Ward Beecher

Without a sense of proportion there can be neither good
taste nor genuine intelligence, nor perhaps moral integrity.

—Eric Hoffer

A truly refined mind will seem to be ignorant of the
existence of anything that is not perfectly proper, placid,
and pleasant.

—Charles Dickens

As a man thinketh, so he is.

—Proverbs 23:7

He who conquers others is strong. He who conquers himself is mighty.

—Lao Tzu

I am, indeed, a king, because I know how to rule myself.

—Pietro Aretino

The beauty of the soul shines out when a man bears with composure one heavy mischance after another, not because he does not feel them, but because he is a man of high and heroic temper.

—Aristotle

Across planes of consciousness, we have to live with the paradox that opposite things can be simultaneously true.

—Ram Dass

Always keep your composure. You can't score from the penalty box; and to win, you have to score.

—Horace

Real knowledge is to know the extent of one's ignorance.

—Confucius

There is nothing either good or bad, but thinking makes it so.

—Shakespeare

No one tests the depth of a river with both feet.

—Ashanti proverb

He who wants a rose must respect the thorn.

—Persian proverb

Seek ye first the good things of the mind, and the rest will either be supplied or its loss will not be felt.

—Francis Bacon

Mind is the forerunner of (all evil) states. Mind is chief; mind-made are they. If one speaks or acts with wicked mind, suffering follows one, even as the wheel follows the hoof of the draught-ox.

—Buddha

Mind is the forerunner of (all good) states. Mind is chief; mind-made are they. If one speaks or acts with pure mind, affection follows one, even as one's shadow that never leaves.

—Buddha

He that of such a height hath built his mind, and reared the dwelling of his thoughts so strong, as neither fear nor hope can shake the frame of his resolved powers; nor all the wind of vanity or malice pierce to wrong his settled peace, or to disturb the same; What a fair seat hath he, from whence he may the boundless wastes and wilds of man survey? Unless above himself he can erect himself, how poor a thing is man!

—Samuel Daniel

The mind is its own place, and in itself can make a heaven of hell, or a hell of heaven.

—Milton

You are today where your thoughts have brought you; you will be tomorrow where your thoughts take you.

—James Allen

The universe is change; our life is what our thoughts make it.

—Marcus Antoninus

○

16. *Flexibility*—the ability to adapt to unforeseeable changes or freely shift among a variety of options as circumstances may require.

A man who hardens his neck after much redirection will suddenly be broken beyond remedy.

—Proverbs 29:1

The hearts of the great can be changed.

—Homer

My opinion is a view I hold until—well until I find out something that changes it.

—Luigi Pirandello

Obstinacy standing alone is the weakest of all things in one whose mind is not possessed by wisdom.

—Aeschylus

Stubbornness and stupidity are twins.

—Sophocles

Cause change and lead. Accept change and survive. Resist change and die.

—Ray Norda

Empty your mind, be formless, shapeless, like water. If you put water into a cup, it becomes the cup. You put water into a bottle, and it becomes the bottle. You put it in a teapot, it becomes the teapot. Now, water can flow or it can crash. Be water, my friend.

—Bruce Lee

○

17. *Positiveness*—the practice of focusing thought and awareness on the aspects of people and circumstances that are good or beneficial, rather than on the aspects that are not.

The greatest revolution of our generation is the discovery that human beings, by changing the inner attitudes of their minds, can change the outer aspects of their lives.

—William James

The person who sends out positive thoughts activates the world around him positively and draws back to himself positive results.

—Norman Vincent Peale

Positive thinking will let you do everything better than negative thinking will.

—Zig Ziglar

If you cannot change your fate, change your attitude.

—Chinese proverb

It is the disposition of the thought that altereth the nature of the thing.

—John Lyly

Pessimism is an excuse for not trying and a guarantee to a personal failure.

—Bill Clinton

○

18. *Assertiveness*—the ability to positively and forthrightly express one's self and desires without becoming overbearing.

Assertive people are the most fun to be around. Unlike passive people they'll say what they want, so you know where they stand. And unlike aggressive people, they won't get upset with you if they don't get it.

—Ray Hardin

Until one is committed, there is hesitancy, the chance to draw back, always ineffectiveness. Concerning all acts of initiative (and creation), there is one elementary truth, the ignorance of which kills countless ideas and splendid plans: That the moment one definitely commits oneself, then Providence moves too. All sorts of things occur to help one that would never otherwise have occurred. A whole stream of events issues from the decision, raising in one's favor all manner of unforeseen incidents and meetings and material assistance, which no man could have dreamed would have come his way. Whatever you can do, or dream you can, begin it. Boldness has genius, power and magic in it. Begin it now.

—Goethe

To know oneself, one should assert oneself.

—Albert Camus

Even if you are on the right track, you'll get run over if you just sit there.

—Will Rogers

Know thyself was written over the portal of the antique world. Over the portal of the new world, "Be thyself" shall be written.

—Oscar Wilde

○

19. *Objectivity*—**the ability to mentally step outside one's own perspective and view things as though through the eyes of another person who does not share one's interests, history, or motivations.**

Every truth has two sides; it is well to look at both, before we commit ourselves to either.

—Aesop

It would be wrong to put friendship before the truth.

—Aristotle

He who knows only his own side of the case, knows little of that.

—John Stuart Mill

Truth is a river that is always splitting up into arms that reunite. Islanded between the arms the inhabitants argue for a lifetime as to which is the main river.

—Cyril Connolly

A stander-by may sometimes, perhaps, see more of the game than he that plays it.

—Jonathan Swift

Listening to both sides of a story will convince you that there is more to a story than both sides.

—Frank Tyger

The human understanding is like a false mirror, which, receiving rays irregularly, distorts and discolors the nature of things by mingling its own nature with it.

—Francis Bacon

Anyone who can handle a needle convincingly can make us see a thread which is not there.

—E.H. Gombrich

20. *Communication*—**the ability to accurately relay and receive information, thoughts, and feelings.**

> The tongue of the wise makes knowledge acceptable, but the mouth of fools spouts folly.
>
> —Proverbs 15:2

> No discussion between two persons can be of any use, until each knows clearly what it is that the other asserts.
>
> —Lewis Carroll

> The art of conversation is the art of hearing as well as of being heard.
>
> —William Hazlitt

> To speak agreeably to him with whom we deal, is more than to speak in good words or in good order.
>
> —Francis Bacon

> Most conversations are simply monologues delivered in the presence of a witness.
>
> —Margaret Millar

> To be able to ask a question clearly is two-thirds of the way to getting it answered.
>
> —John Ruskin

Talking is like playing on the harp; there is as much in laying the hands on the strings to stop their vibration as in twanging them to bring out their music.

—Oliver Wendell Holmes

The difference between a smart man and a wise man is that a smart man knows what to say, a wise man knows whether or not to say it.

—Frank M. Garafola

○

21. *Awareness*—**the ability to hold within one's attention, the attributes of their environment and inner state.**

The test of a civilized person is first self-awareness, and then depth after depth of sincerity in self-confrontation.

—Clarence Day

He then learns that in going down into the secrets of his own mind he has descended into the secrets of all minds.

—Emerson

If one does not know to which port one is sailing, no wind is favorable.

—Seneca

There is no greater delight than to be conscious of sincerity on self-examination.

—Confucius

The unexamined life is worth nothing.

—Plato

The world is our school for self-discovery.

—Paul Brunton

Know thyself.

—Socrates

It is wisdom to know others; it is enlightenment to know one's self.

—Lao-Tzu

Self-awareness gives you the capacity to learn from your mistakes as well as your successes. It enables you to keep growing.

—Larry Bossidy and Ram Charan

The most successful people are those who don't have any illusions about who they are. They know themselves well and they can move in the direction of their best talents. They know the kind of culture they thrive in and how they can benefit from that culture. Unfortunately, most people don't understand themselves. Most people don't want to lose their illusions about themselves, although they say they want to take charge of their career.

—Bud Bray

Everything that irritates us about others can lead us to an understanding of ourselves.

—Carl Jung

When we're identified with Awareness, we're no longer living in a world of polarities. Everything is present at the same time.

—Ram Dass

It's all real and it's all illusory: that's Awareness.

—Ram Dass

Notes

1. As quoted in "The Philosophy of Niels Bohr" by Aage Petersen, *Bulletin of the Atomic Scientists*, 19: 7 (September 1963), under Wikiquote, http://en.wikiquote.org/wiki/Niels_Bohr.

2. Max Tegmark and John Archibald Wheeler, "100 Years of Quantum Mysteries," *Scientific American*, February 2001, http://www.scientificamerican.com/article.cfm?id=100-years-of-quantum-mysteries.

3. Alan Lightman, "Relativity and the Cosmos." *NOVA: Einstein's Big Idea*, http://www.pbs.org/wgbh/nova/einstein/relativity/.

4. Daniel Styer, et al. "Nine Formulations of Quantum Mechanics," *American Journal of Physics* 70, no. 3 (2002), 297, http://www-physique.u-strasbg.fr/cours/l3/divers/meca_q_hervieux/Articles/Nine_form.pdf.

5. Richard P. Feynman, "Lecture 6: Probability and Uncertainty—the Quantum Mechanical View of Nature: On the Apparent Absurdities of Quantum Behavior," *The Character of Physical Law* (Cambridge, Massachusetts: MIT Press, 1967).

6. Niels Bohr, BrainyQuote.com, Xplore Inc, 2010, http://www.brainyquote.com/quotes/quotes/n/nielsbohr384378.html, accessed April 12, 2010.

7. Lynne McTaggart, *The Intention Experiment* (New York: Free Press, 2008), xv.

8. George F. Will, "A Debate That Does Not End," *Newsweek*, July 4, 2005.

9. Phil Anderson, "Re: New Paper: 2-Connections on 2-Bundles," The String Coffee Table: A Group Blog on Physics, December 30, 2004, http://golem.ph.utexas.edu/string/archives/000488.html.

10. Sheldon Glashow, "Viewpoints on String Theory," *NOVA: The Elegant Universe*, http://www.pbs.org/wgbh/nova/elegant.

11. P.A.M. Dirac, *The Principles of Quantum Mechanics* (Oxford, England: Oxford University Press, 1930).

12. Peter Medawar, "Two Conceptions of Science," *The Strange Case of the Spotted Mice and Other Classic Essays on Science* (Oxford, England: Oxford University Press, 1961).

13. Roy H. Williams, "Quantum Quotes," Trumpet
Universe, Unseen Worlds, http://www.trumpetuniverse.org/
unseenworlds.html.

14. McTaggart, xv.

15. Joseph LeDoux, *Synaptic Self: How Our Brains Become
Who We Are* (New York: Penguin, 2002).

16. "The Law Against Slavery," BBC, under "Ethics Guide,"
http://www.bbc.co.uk/ethics/slavery/modern/law.shtml.

17. Ibid.

18. Jeffrey D. Sachs, *The End of Poverty—Economic
Possibilities for Our Time* (New York: Penguin Group, 2006), 3.

19. Ibid., xvii.

20. Worldwatch Institute, "State of The World 2004:
Consumption by the Numbers," January 8, 2004, http://www.
worldwatch.org/node/1783.

21. Ibid.

22. McTaggart, 32.

23. Ibid., xxix.

24. Ibid.

25. Ibid., 51.

26. Ibid., 30.

27. Ibid., 79.

28. Ibid.,

29. Ibid., 26.

30. McTaggart, 32. The author is commenting on William A. Tiller's *Science and Human Transformation* (Walnut Creek, CA, Pavior Publishing, 1997), 196.

31. McTaggart, 71.

32. Ibid., 73.

33. Ibid.

34. Paraphrased from Abraham Maslow, *Motivation and Personality*. 2nd ed. (New York: Harper & Row, 1970).

35. Ibid.

36. Thomas J. Stanley, *The Millionaire Mind* (Kansas City, Kansas: Andrews McMeel Publishing, 2000), 21.

37. Ibid., 61.

38. Ibid.

39. Ibid.

40. Ibid., 61-62.

41. Ibid., 187.

42. Ben Franklin, *Autobiography of Benjamin Franklin* (New York: Henry Holt and Company, 1916).